Lily of the Valley, Romance of Souls

by

Rebecca Lebron

Lily of the Valley,
Romance of Souls

Copyright © 2021 by Rebecca Lebron

MAPLE LEAF PUBLISHING INC.
3rd Floor 4915 54 St Red Deer,
Alberta T4N 2G7 Canada
General Inquiries & Customer Service
Phone: 1-(403)-356-0255
Toll Free: 1-(888)-498-9380
Email: info@mapleleafpublishinginc.com

ISBN:
Paperback: 978-1-77419-088-3
eBook: 978-1-77419-089-0

Contents

Dedication

I dedication this book to my children Zanifa and Jamal with joy, appreciation, and love.

About the Author

Rebecca Lebron was born Rebecca Fletcher in Trinidad, West Indies.

In a poverty-stricken village, she disliked her life and vowed when she grew up to change her life and leave her birth country.

A young mother of two children, she immigrated to the United States, in Brooklyn, New York. There she worked as a home health aide, struggling many times. She could not pay her rent or buy food and clothes.

Then one day something changed within her soul. An idea came to her mind. She wrote this book.

As a child she loved to make jewelry with sea shells and electric wires. In addition, she loved to draw roses, make hats and handbags, etc. She also loved to write, but whenever her parents saw her writing, she would get a beating because they thought she was writing to boys. They would say to her, "You're no good."

She would hide her writing by sitting on it or tearing it into pieces. One time she chewed up her writing, which was on a small piece of paper, and swallowed it, taking her beating, knowing there were something more and better in life that she was born to do.

Acknowledgments

I wish to thank God for giving me such a gift to share with the world and getting my attention when I was too busy working, by slowing me down when I almost broke my knee so I could complete this book.

To my daughter, for typing the manuscript and who with patience and endurance stood by me. Thank you.

Introduction

Dream vision, a voice whispered. The name Lily of the Valley is about the mind, body, heart, spirit, and soul. The heavenly holy beings that whispered from the since I was five years old, I have seen, heard, and made conversation with them. Their wisdom is knowledge and medicine to my soul. Their holy power is alive, real, and beautiful. I'm always grateful and thankful every time I begin and end a chapter. Their guidance takes me where they want me to go, so I can explore and be creative at that time, unleashing my creativity that unlocks the wisdom which I had obtained in my ancient past lives that have been hidden within my soul.

Chapter 1

Whisper

Hush! Listen to the wind-what do you hear? A whisper, whispering in the wind. You can't hear anything, but I can hear something, that voice without a face. It has a soul but no race or color. A sweet-sounding voice, connecting to each soul in the universe, creating inward authentic powers of love, kindness, and honesty. Listen! One can really hear its divine intervention and interaction with our souls. The sensational wisdom creates a rewarding passion in the souls of those of us here on planet earth, the whisper that bonds the heart and soul of every living creature. Sometime we may fall and the whisper may take us places we have never been before, show us things we have never seen, heard, or knew existed. The very whisper we are afraid of, that's the whisper that may guide us to the right path.

My hand is on my heart. I can hear her whisper saying, "No more." A young girl with long dark hair and wearing pink jeans with a green sweater top is walking on her way to wherever she is going, saying to herself, "I surely had enough."

A man packing his luggage on a tour bus is telling his buddies he is leaving this town. The whisper echoed in his ear. Can you recognize your whisper guiding the forces of your intention to exist with an effect that is so powerful in the universe it may contradict one's mind, but stimulate the soul.

The spirit is the outer layer, like the petal of the lily that floats on the Valley lake. The heart of the lily is the heart of the soul. It can take you beyond the greatest level of powers that any human soul can imagine; it cultivates the spirit that feeds the soul. The soul needs food like our body needs food to stay alive, spiritual food revives one's spirit. One must become aware of with what you nourish the soul. Everyone has or had some kind of affliction and anguish in their soul; almost everyone leaves this world with their hearts broken.

What you feed your soul with there is no substitute. The spiritual food will sustain your soul, speeding roots, and taking up residence in the very depths of your soul. Whether it's good or evil, it may bring blessings in abundance or curses in abundance that fill your life with joy and happiness or hurt and anger. Don't let your soul become like the restless wind, not knowing what direction it will sway. Understand that the soul needs a purpose. Look at it as an adventure. Trust in your whisper. It will bring you hope and inspiration, like the fresh and healthy crops sprouting in the fields, each one a spiritual adventure traveling on an extraordinary, amazing trip, gathering knowledge to store in the soul. Be true to the soul. It's the must honest and strongest part of any living being in the universe. In the spirit world is the key to the golden gates, where chariots await us for the ever-lasting blessing we so hungrily yearn for, like the edible white rose with a single pink petal in the garden of Eden which heals the soul.

Come, my little one, don't be overwhelmed with anxiety of your whisper. There's hope and dreams of what lies ahead for you; the message is in your whisper. It's the prayers of your heart, the answer is in your soul. So many questions and very little answers. I crept into my bed refocusing for what seemed as one silent moment listening to my fears of how discouraged I felt, so hurt and reflecting, too scared to speak my mind. Pulling the covers over me, my heart sank while tears came rolling down my cheeks like the dew drops rolling off the lily leaf, drop by drop. My fear is intense and in my distress the whispering voice hears my cry, I'm trying to listen without becoming defensive or blaming others, but fears of abandonment have been with me all my life. As a child I learned to conceal it to survive, and it's killing my soul. Every time I try to reach out there is a feeling of guilt. My human emotion is strong and tries to destroy my spirit, burning so much energy that is a part of me as the blood that run through my veins.

I can hear this distant whisper inside me. What I had once thought or as weakness becomes my strength, minute by minute. No screaming or pleading, not even grinding my teeth. It's no game. One must be the master of one's own whisper. It keeps me grounded with a kinder, calmer spirit. Everyone is intuitive. Tap into your intuition by being aware of your whisper.

One day a little old lady crossing the street heard her whisper. She hesitated and stopped almost in the middle of the street when she heard her grandson's voice. She then turned around to wave goodbye to him. To her amazement he wasn't in sight; seconds later, there was a loud screeching as two cars collided. The universe puts things the way they are supposed to be, and if over time something doesn't happen, that's a lesson which teaches us something about ourselves. We all must learn to listen to our whisper.

Chapter 2

Seta

Seta, a young Indian woman, was pushing a stroller holding her newborn baby boy, Ramish, her twelve-year-old daughter Mala walking by her side, fleeing from their home. She was tired of bad treatment from her family. Seta was a single parent who lives with her younger siblings and her parents. She fell in love with a rich young man from the Middle East. When she became with child, Sherif, the young man, sent her and their unborn child away to Seta's homeland, penniless and homeless. Sherif and Seta came from two different countries. They met each other in London, England. Seta couldn't stay in England. She was on a three-month vacation and had overstayed.

Sherif never stood up as a man to fight his family. Seta tried to protect him from his family because he was afraid of them. In the end she served time in jail. Sherif came to visit her a few times and bought a one-way ticket without her knowing it for her and their unborn child. Seven months with child, she was deported from England.

Seta and her unborn child were yet to discover that their lives would be a living hell for many years to come. She believed that one day Sherif would come to rescue them. She waited and waited in anticipation for the love of her life to come to embrace his family. Tension was building up in her mind. Every month she would sit by the little window in a darkened room waiting for the mailman to come so she could receive her letter with a check for the amount of four hundred pounds from Sherif.

Seta's family didn't have a phone or running water, not even indoor plumbing. They were dirt poor. She never believed in her heart that Sherif abandoned them, but in reality he did. She lived in her own shadow of belief for years. After a few years the letters stopped coming and Sherif never came to their rescue. She didn't listen to her whisper when it told her to take the journey away from her village and start a new life for herself and her daughter.

Seta's second child, baby Ramish, belonged to another young man. She thought they would have a life together. She wanted to belong to someone, to feel wanted and special. She longed for a real love but Hosa lived a shady life, Seta had no idea until it was too late. When over the course of time one may takes a wrong path, step back into your own footprint and deny your own soul its pathway.

Hosa loved her in his own messed-up way. They both had unresolved issues and harbored resentment in their hearts for the opposite sex as well as fears of abandonment. He was a rambling fool who kept running through the bushes, and she was an emotionally naive young fool who expected too much from Hosa. All Seta ever received from him was unpleasantness and intense grief, afraid to listen to her whisper.

Early one morning, dressed in her best bright, colorful outfit, which was red and gold. Seta looked into the minor, saying to herself, I have always imagined my soul mate to be standing by myside. Turning her head, she looked at her two children, four-month-old Ramish still asleep on the dirty wood floor, laying on a blanket full of holes chewed up by mice. Her daughter Mala sat in a corner with her knees pulled up to her chest, her arms wrapped around her knees, rocking back and forth. Seta clasped her hands, closed her eyes, and cried out loud, "Help me, my creator! I need you so much and feel the walls closing in on me." In that moment she felt the loneliest of all as her tears were streaming down her face like a stream of water running down from the rooftop. She began bawling her eyes out.

Slowly walking as the floor creaked at every step she took toward her daughter, without a spoken word Seta reached out her hand. Mala Stood up, took her mother's hand, and they both walked to the window and looked up to heaven in silence, then walked back to Seta's tiny corner in their tiny bedroom in the family house. Ransacking a cardboard box where she kept their belongings, she pulled out a white t-shirt with pink hearts on the front and a pink ankle-length skirt for Mala to wear. They had no shoes, only a pair of worn-out dirty-looking rubber flip-flops. Baby Ramish wore a hand-me-down jumper, which he had out-grown. The white and yellow jumper looked so faded and dingy.

Seta whispered to herself and looked up to the ceiling that was cracked with peeling paint and water-stain marks caused by the heavy rain that fell two weeks ago. Her voice was soft. Hanging her head, she said, "My creator, look at me. I come to you with heavy feet, a heavy heart, and a weary soul. My body is aching from this hard life, my spirit is broken, my soul sometimes feels lost, and my eyelids are heavy. They can hardly keep open. I'm tired of looking and waiting,"

Taking her two children, she walked out of the bedroom, closing the door behind her as if to close what bad memories she had in that room. Her family was at the breakfast table. She and her two children slipped out without anyone noticing, Seta and her children were gone and no one cared whether they were gone or not.

Well, I must have done something wrong in a past life. Seta talked a lot to herself. That way no one could curse or yell at her. She walked down the stairs from the

13

family's big old one-story house, baby Ramish in one arm, stroller in the other, Mala two steps ahead with one change of clothes for each of them. The baby had been drinking formula made with arrowroot and starch boiled in water and sugar, for months, with no help from his father.

Seta had a job as a dishwasher in a restaurant and had been saving some of her money for two years so they could leave the small village where she grew up. She wanted better for her two children, and two hundred dollars was all she had. She stood at the end of the stairs as the family dog came running at Mala's feet. Lala was his name. When he was a pup Mala would clap her hands, saying, "La, la, la!" He would come running, wagging his tail, so she named him Lala. He sensed something was wrong and he started barking, which sounded as if he was crying. Mala patted Lala on his head and said to him, "We are leaving. You can't come with us. Take care of Grandma and Grandpa, my aunts and uncles, okay! We love you." She hugged Lala so tight his tongue stuck out.

Seta's heart was breaking as they walked away to what they thought was going to be a better life for them. She didn't share her plans with anyone. Her heart was pounding so loud that she could hear it in her chest. She felt a bit shaky. Closing her eyes, she stood for a moment with her head hanging, then lifted her head up high and walked away, detaching from everything and everyone she left behind. It's my family and my life. Things will get better in time to come. Being afraid and yet determined, she took the path, not knowing what to expect.

The hardship and loneliness was more than even her heart could bear. Each heart-breaking thought deepened her sense of desolation and she felt the need to connect with someone. What could I do? Seta asked herself. Oh. Well, one day I will be successful in life. She never let a guy get too close to her heart. All she dreamt of was to have a successful life for herself and her two children, not because of what had happened to her, but because of how she reacted to what happened to her.

Seta learned whenever darkness threatens to over-whelm us to look up to heaven and you will see a ray of light. Follow the light. Look wherever love glows on any face. Hope will uplift your spirit. Courage will define all other human behavior. In desperation, call on the creator. Look into your soul. Fear, anger, hate, and sorrow will turn into compassion and patience. Always remember to ask for help when needed, accept help when offered, but most of all, listen to your whisper, it comes from your soul.

No one knew Seta cried a lot in the shadows with tears trickling down her face. She listened to the steady rhythm of her hem beating and laughs out loud, saying, "As long as we are alive, pain will speed in and out of our lives. My mind is clear and I feel reassured I'll be able to make it through whatever lies ahead." The whisper, maybe a voice or a feeling deep inside your soul, may come in a dream vision or a waking vision. You should find the courage to listen and then do what you need to. It warms the heart and heals the soul. Even if the feeling or voice may be frightening or painful, be brave. The best is waiting in the distance.

Chapter 3

An Idea

Many of us have ideas, but how many make their idea come to life? Every idea and person in this universe is valuable. It does not matter if we are of different generations, different cultures, or religions. Some people have big ideas, small ideas, good ideas, or bad ideas. It makes you feel like a kid in a candy store. It lights up your eyes. Your brain begins thinking, asking so many questions: What? How? Why? Yes? No? Now or maybe later? As if you were going through the pages of a book while your fingers get the energy to reach out and start working, transforming the idea beneath your hands.

Appreciating all the little things so much more, your eyes cherish every little outline and color. It consumes your mind, body, heart, spirit, and soul. You sleep, eat, and breathe your idea. Do you understand there's no escape? You can run, but it will conquer the sense of your inner being, centering your inner thoughts on your idea.

Imaging someone unwrapping a gift. You can see the amazing look on their face, the eyes widening, a happy wide smile appearing on their face, then returning to their own little world. When that gift means everything to that person, ask someone what they think their answer may be. It's great not really understanding the deepness of your concept, some not even caring. Behind that idea there is a greater power and determination that pushes the unseen forces, which taps you on the shoulder every now and then combines with this universe, contacting your soul, relating and lending their expertise to human beings in their minds. Their visions and knowledge came from their ancient past lives to be researched in modern ways that make us become more accustomed to introducing our ideas to the world. Whether it's painting, writing, inventing, or whatever your idea may be, someone may find something in it that deeply interests them.

I am an inventor, I also design jewelry, perfume, and handbags, and I am writing this book. My ideas came in my dream visions. My inner thoughts compelled me to put my ideas on paper. It felt like a thorn in my side. I was a little skittish at first, avoiding it for many months, until it became intolerable. My soul couldn't take the emotional turmoil I was putting my mind through. Once I put the ideas on paper my soul became free and everything fell into place.

To me it was one of the longest walks in my life. The faster I walked, the more I walked, the slower I got to my destination. They told me, "Be patient. It will be rewarding when you get there and a feast to your eyes," but I'm still waiting. My toughest battle yet is finding manufacturers to make my products.

An inventor sees the same things others see in different ways. Perhaps it may need improving or they see the world needs something new that will make life easier and at the same time change the world. Being creative in many ways takes inspiration, motivation, perseverance, and a deep inner strength coming from one's soul.

Chapter 4

The Valley Field

The valley field is this world; the lake in the valley is our body. The lily in the valley lake is our soul. Our body houses our soul, which lives in this world. The master of all masters is our creator who lives in our soul, quenching our spiritual thirst. If the valley field is destroyed, the lake in the valley will be sad. The lily in the valley lake will have to work very hard with the help of our creator to encourage the lake to stay alive in the valley field. We are living beings of life. If the soul stays too long without spiritual food from our creator, the soul will be lost. It will wilt and dry up like the lily, and if our foundation rocks beneath us, getting courage we never knew we had. It's the wealth of our souls.

A special gift, wisdom, is the sixth sense. The creator approved it with the purpose of learning the lessons of the emotional, intimate melody of love, with understanding, trust, and confidence. Deep into our heart and soul it enriches and sustains us through life. Spiritual growth makes us grow as human beings. It's like remembering to take our vitamins. The creator is love. We all need this wisdom in our lily. Let the wisdom in our lily float from one lake to another until the end of time and beyond.

We live and we die. Don't be stiff hearted. When the clock ticks and time runs out that is all the time we were meant to have in this dimension. By renewing our spiritual thoughts and replenishing our hearts and souls, we all are capturing the freshness of the lily floating as the wind blows from the mountaintops while it ripples the water in the lake below, where the lily stands in the lily of the valley. Discover the true, natural feeling and the pureness of spiritual joy that will uplift the spirit and clean the soul.

Let the lily in the valley guide us through the rhythm of life from the womb to the tomb. It will see us through the journey of life until our time to exit this world and we have come to the end of our journey. We must see in others the goodness within their souls, and value our time and ourselves. Embrace each soul with kindness and love as if it is the last time, for we never know when our mission will be accomplished and it's time to leave this life.

Chapter 5

The Lady's Man

Big Kirk loves high thrills. He has a fickle mind and shifty eyes. He is also very tall, over six feet. When Carmen met Kirk, the first things that caught her attention were his sad blue eyes and his height. Her pleasant smile caught his eye; he was mesmerized by her big, brown, beautiful smiling eyes, her charming personality, and her laugh.

Kirk, a white American, and Carmen, a black Caribbean mixed native, set off a sort of affair. They were both married but Carmen was separated. To them it was the most rewarding feeling they ever had. They connected instantly. Their first kiss was tantalizing and exciting, absolutely breathtaking. Two months went by without seeing each other. Their feelings grew for each other and one can't outrun love. Sooner or later it overcomes you, especially when the heart always wants what it can't have.

Carmen had yet to know that Kirk developed an obsession to manipulate, which caused her dumfounding grief. Kirk had already been seeing another for many years outside his marriage, but told Carmen he had never been unfaithful to his wife, Anna, that he always followed the yellow brick road home. Carmen smelled something fishy. At the time her mind was preoccupied with meaningless thinking. The only problem with such a perfect story is that it was to good too be true and Carmen told herself Kirk was only blowing smoke up her skirt.

The next time they saw each other he told her the same story again. She was astonished and stunned to watch Kirk look her in the eyes and lie without fumbling, which made her think he had told the same lies many times before with a double tongue. He was a hunter and loved a good chase. Carmen was his prey. His lies were so compelling. At first there were no telltale signs that were recognizable, but the prompting of her inner self and her intuitive mind convinced her Kirk was not all that he was pretending to be.

Carmen's world was rocked and her trust in him began to seem like evil conspirators determined to undermine him. As time went by she uncovered a few more lies. Lies have a way of surfacing through deceit and denial; sometimes muzzled truth grows ferocious.

Kirk had a way to be honest about lying and Carmen had a way to be deceitful by letting him think she believed he was telling her the truth. We are supposed to know the truth in our brain. The soul knows everything in the universe. The things that are real we can't change. His lies and secrets were carefully planned and destructive, but when Carmen looked at him she saw a man who needed love. The heart sees only what it wants to see and can deal with. This was a terrible betrayal, when her feelings were growing for him and his were deep for her, too. Big Kirk broke it off with Carmen and for three years he stalked her. They both thought about each other every so often and missed the opportunity to know each other. One day Kirk made a surprise return to Carmen. She decided to teach him a lesson, that the shadow of his past was about to come to light and she would be the last woman he would ever hurt or use again. He was a scorpion among women and needed to be treated the way he treated women, dropping him in midair, leaving the aching pain of love in his heart with his tail dragging, for playing her for a fool.

Kirk was a womanizer who was having an affair with Candace right under his wife's nose. Both women got along well with each other. Anna was not aware of her husband's affair with his employees in his office. No one suspected that the relationship was anchored. They were one happy, working family. Anna was a woman who had her head high in the clouds and her nose burried in the mud, whose eyes were wide shut and who didn't tune into her inner voice. It may be hard to face and doesn't always bring resolution. Trust in the truth because one person's courage is another one's strength.

Kirk had a dark magnetic pull on those who should have known but didn't that he cared for Candace and thought she was in love with him. She was also married. Kirk told Carmen he had everything he wanted, including money and plenty of it, so he could go back and forth when he wanted to. He was a lost soul, who was swimming in a tank, round and round, who stole women's hearts then ran. Carmen got sucked between floors. She opened her heart to Kirk and he stuck a knife into it. He wanted her to love him. It played out how he wanted it but deep in her soul she knew he was in love with her, too. She also believed that the reason they met each other was no co-incidence. They had the same birth month, only one year apart. The purpose was for her to learn to open her heart and trust again and for him to be real with himself and others, to stop decorating himself with unnecessary lies.

The short times they shared together were cherished moments, something you can only see when you open up your heart. There is good in each soul; someone special will find it. She also learned not to let love blind you from the things you need to know and see. Looking into someone's eyes is the window to their soul. She should have remembered that love starts in the heart and comes through the eyes. If it's right, your soul will let you know or your heart will move on to someone else until you find the right someone.

Carmen also believed Kirk was her angel messenger who was sent to light up her life and give her hope. There would be a rainbow behind the dark cloud, love that she could feel in the depths of her soul, inspiration so she could find her willpower to stop feeling suffocated and stumbling through life. He was her sunlight, helping her out of the darkness and the blanket of love that warmed her heart. Big Kirk calmed her spirit, soothed her soul, and healed wounded heart. She could tell that life would be forever different. That was the goodness Carmen saw in big Kirk's heart and soul. They both made a path that if they couldn't be together in this lifetime they would be together in the next life. They had an affair of the soul, mind, spirit, and heart, which was very intense and deep into their souls with the essence of the universe. He touched her heart, awakened her spirit, and opened her eyes; they will forever love each other deep into their souls.

Chapter 6

Judging Others

The universe sees each one of us as equal. There is no reason for the universe to pass judgment on anyone. It considers each soul special. It has a special purpose for a limited time.

Early one morning as old man Johnson was taking his walk, which he had done for the past fifteen years, two teenage boys were arguing about a girl named Shannon. The two boys attended the same high school in Flushing, Queens, New York. Kevin and Curtis were best friends. Curtis and his family had moved to New York from Atlanta, Georgia. This was his first time here in the big city, where everything seemed so different. The buildings were so big and tall. People were always busy on the street; they talked fast and loud and were always in a hurry. He worried that life here in New York City would be too much for him to handle, and missed his hometown in Georgia.

Curtis heard a soul crying out behind him. In every shadow there is a light and a waterfall of blessing. Don't judge what you haven't seen or know. Don't be like an icy waterfall. All you need is a little courage. He was feeling withdrawn; he looked at all the different faces. This is my neighborhood. I need a friend and I have to find a new best friend.

"Listen, buddy," his father said gruffly, "It's okay, Curtis. Let's take a ride." They took a ride on the downtown train. The train stopped at every station so the ride seemed to take forever. Curtis liked riding on the subway and listening to the wheels screeching on the track. They watched people get on and off each stop. Some passengers held on to the rail. The horn honked as the train pulled out of the station. A kid standing next to him on the train stepped on a guy's foot. He said, "Sorry, man," and moved to the opposite side of the train car. Curtis looked straight at him. The kid said, "What up?" At the next station they got off. The kid

introduced himself to Curtis. "Hi, I'm Kevin," and "I'm Curtis and I'm here from Atlanta, Georgia." Their friendship began. The expression on Kevin's face was bright when he found out that they lived in the same neighborhood. After that day they were seen together in Kevin's Uncle Daniel's grocery store on Main Street.

One day he walked with Curtis to buy a loaf of bread and a gallon of milk. Curtis and Kevin were standing in the same line. Shannon walked toward them and she smiled. Kevin said, "Hi, Shannon. "What's up, girl? You're looking so fine with your bad self."

She looked at Kevin with an attitude, then said, "Who is your friend?"

"He said, "Curtis, and he is from Georgia."

"Hi, Curtis, I'm Shannon."

Kevin said to Shannon, "Watch it, girl."

Shannon said, "Talk to the hand." She was a with a New York attitude and also a hottie. Kevin liked that about Shannon.

The three became best friends. It was an interracial friendship, Curtis was black, Spanish and Greek; Kevin was Russian, Chinese, and native American; and Shannon was black, white, and French descended. Their friendship lasted for a very long time, until one day Curtis thought Shannon was taking drugs and stealing to support her habit. He confided in Kevin, who gave Curtis a noogie on his head, then confronted Shannon. She denied it. For weeks her friends kept their distance from her, believing only what they wanted to believe.

The truth was she was never on any kind of substance. Neither Kevin or Curtis ever visited her home, nor did she ever invite them over. Shannon was so ashamed of the lifestyle her family lived, the suffering that comes from not being able to have enough to eat, drink, or pay bills. Her parents were poor and needy. Her mother worked two jobs, retail and housekeeping, and her father was on permanent disability. She felt powerless over the fear that was so devastating day after day, wondering when they would be kicked out of their home. The thought of being homeless made Shannon sick to her stomach from the fear of going into greater suffering. She panicked and gasped for breath. Her soul and body could no longer endure the hunger. If Kevin and Curtis knew the truth. how would they react? She was too ashamed to let them know. Shannon cried out, "No, it's important to me that I do what I must to help out at home even if it means stealing to survive." The words came to her mind that her family didn't come into this world to struggle in life and death. Months went by as she drifted further away from Kevin and Curtis. She told them that they were friends, but neither of them ever had enough trust or faith in her.

One Monday morning Kevin saw how melancholy Shannon looked and asked if he could walk with her after school. She said, "Yes, only if you listen to what I have to say." "Okay," Kevin said. She had more fire in her than anyone he had known and he missed her friendship. She apologized for what had happened and explained about her life. Kevin believed Shannon; she was relieved that the truth was revealed. He also apologized for judging her without facts and that he would help her figure out a way she could help her family without stealing. He would ask his Uncle Daniel if he would hire Shannon to work at the grocery store after school.

The next day when Curtis saw that Kevin and Shannon were friends again, he felt angry, sad, and stunned. All alone, walking around without his friends. he was confused about why. Curtis wished they all could become friends again, telling stories that flowed like the water falls in heaven. His heart pounded. The sweat from his eyebrows ran down the side of his face. It was the moment of his own truth as he fiddled with this thumbs. How could he have judged Shannon without ever really knowing her? One could see the hurt in his eye and the sadness in his soul. Curtis told his father Joe, who told him, "You must never swallow everything you hear about others. Judge without facts or embrace it. Don't let anyone steal your confidence in yourself or others. See others through your own eyes. When you hear something, don't let your mind take off like planes on a runway or your mouth run like a motor. You have to stop and think for you never know, someday it may be you."

Chapter 7

Haven

I found my haven in Woodhaven, New York. The feeling to move from place to place in New York City kept pulling at my heartstrings heavily. Maybe it was a leap of faith; at the time it was hard to explain and became the strongest feeling in the universe for me, mysteriously intense and crystal clear. A cheerful lighthearted song to my soul.

Yesterday I felt awkward and uncomfortable stepping out of the building where I lived with my family and paused, looking around for just a second. That is when I knew for sure it was time to move out of Brooklyn. It struck a chord in me that changed everything. I remember thinking it would be nice if I could find a community where I felt I belonged. Coming to Woodhaven was the coming of the dawn for me.

The minute we came near the outskirts of the neighborhood I knew in my soul this was where I was supposed to be. There was no second-guessing, I was certain within my soul I had reached my destination and that this was my moment. After moving into the neighborhood early one morning, I looked out the bedroom window. The first thing that caught my eyes was the name Woodhaven on a sign pole. Oh, was this my little haven? Not only in my mind, it was in my spirit, my soul, my heart, and even in my bones, an inner peace.

We all search for some kind of haven in our life. When it is found it is as if sweet angels sing with heavenly voices through our souls. No one wants to feel invisible or stifled by the life they live or by living in a marriage that isn't working, no matter how hard you try to hold it together. I had been living in a place I no longer felt it was right for me repeating the same old mistakes and patterns over and over again. Why was I allowing myself to be treated this way? And why was I doing this to my life? I had to make a decision, to stay entangled in this marriage or to set myself free. Memorizing these words gave me the courage to get out for good, even burning that bridge behind me.

I have cried and I waited with the rhythm of my heart and soul for the day when the tension became silent and I was calm enough to know what the universe wanted me to know that I wasn't paying attention to. What was I afraid of? Being an immigrant, one can be taken advantage of. I came to America in the early eighties and got married in the early nineties. Shortly after, the marriage began to go downhill. Refusing to face the fact that I was in harm's way, it was the toughest time for me. The shame, pain, cruelty, and disgrace I had to endure was more than most human beings could withstand.

The universe doesn't forget, like us human beings, when we do harm to others, even if we think in our minds that it was the right thing to do. In the heat of the moment and if the universe didn't see it that way, you can bet one day later down the road when we forget all about our harmful acts to another the universe will let us have it, doing unto us much later in life and much worse. Don't get me wrong, for the universe is very forgiving, unlike humans. If we do good to others we will reap the rewards with the same forces, like a bird singing in our life. At an early age I always had to be doing something for someone else's sake. If I didn't stop doing to survive and live, when or how would I know to just live life? Instead of surviving, when would I know what living is? In the end every one would lead their own lives and I'd be left alone, wishing for what should have been with remorse and regret.

Listening to the chatter inside my head it occurred to me that it was time to change the course of my life, while the clock kept ticking, not knowing when it would stop with my own sorrows as well as ongoing support from friends. Woodhaven, Queens, New York, became my breathing space, like a child running along the green park, racing throughout the curve of trees, enjoying freedom. Coming to New York was the end of a previous lifetime. I completed that journey in the year 2002 and I have begun the new cycle of another past lifetime. The end of an old and the beginning of a new, which is the awakening of a new soul in this lifetime, but an ancient soul from a past life.

Chapter 8

Miracle

Imagine you are making your own recipe. You know what the ingredients are, at what time to put them in and whether to fold, mix, whisk, or shake, and what is the last ingredient to add to bring out the flavor you want. Life is like a recipe and a guiding line. We were conceived, then born into this world. We live however we want to, and then we die. Dying is the final ingredient of this life and the beginning to another pathway to the afterlife, where life continues not of this human flesh, but of the spirit and of the soul. Some souls become spirit guides. Others reincarnate to help souls who need to find their way toward the heavenly fountains, washing and cleansing, purifying and preparing the unclean souls to be welcomed in heaven. They also receive the souls that are leaving this dimension. That is part of the cycle and miracle of life. There is no limitation in the spirit world. Those who guide souls all stand at the entrance of the heavenly fountain, while others wash, then prepare and anoint the souls, leading them to the pathway where every soul will enter into orientation before meeting with the heavenly creator. They are then shuttled off to another entrance where they will wait their turn to become spirit guides or to be reincarnated.

There are many spirit guides for many different reasons. The day we are conceived, a spirit guide is appointed to us and remains with us until the day we die, then that spirit guide is given to a newborn life. Some may have more than one spirit guide; some people call them "Angels" or "Saints," while others may have one and not be aware. No human being in this world is without a spirit guide. They are helpers of the creator with his blessing and guidance, making miracles come true.

Sarah and Mindy are twin sisters; both have the same spirit guide. It is possible for others to have the same spirit guide (angel). Wherever they were, both sisters lived a life of sadness, loneliness, and tribulation. One night their spirit guide,

whom they called Joshua, appeared in a dream to Sarah, these were his words: "Sarah, God's peace and blessing be unto you. May the Lord shower his eternal mercy upon his children in this world, keeping all safe, everyone throughout this year and the years to come. Tell Mindy her dark trials and sorrows are about to come to an end. Yours also. You are one family stick it out together, with God's divine grace." The spirit guide waited until their body, mind, heart, soul, and spirit were broken, but humble, and they were about to lock their hearts for the rest of their lives. Spirit guide Joshua opened his hand, blowing the breath of heavenly hope and blessing upon them and their families.

They had to learn their lessons of patience and humbleness by paying their dues. Both Sarah and Mindy became humble servants of the creator. Both also appreciated knowing and having their spirit guide Joshua when their days were hopeless and the nights were darkened and lonely. He watched over them. When their tears came pouring down uncontrollably like rain, he caught every drop in his heavenly hands and held it tightly, then consoled their aching hearts.

The sisters' days of darkness, trials, and grief didn't go unnoticed by God and their spirit guide Joshua. Now they are reaping the rewards of happiness and prosperity in abundance To Sarah and Mindy, it was a miracle.

When all their hopes and were almost gone the spirit guide (angel) of miracles came to their rescue. What is your miracle?

Chapter 9

Please Step Forward

((Come! Open your hearts only for a moment," the universe speaks all on board. "Please step forward. Why are you here and why are you stepping forward?"

Amber and Andrew were newlyweds growing together and growing apart. In our hearts forever and in our souls, a deep peace dances with wisdom. Both Amber and Andrew wanted to go on a spiritual retreat. Amber wondered how far heaven was. It between the earth and the sky or beyond the sky? What really is beyond that big blue sky that our physical eyes can't see? How far is the Sky? Refocusing her attention, she knew that God was in control and he knew best, that we must wait silently with patience and with courage.

Heaven is a world like a planet that these earthly eyes can't see. No one of human flesh can enter into the kingdom of God. Only our souls really know how get there and what it is like, but choose not to let this earthly mind remember. Our souls yearn for its heavenly home, but we all have to wait until he calls us to go home, then our souls will allow our spirit and mind to remember where and how far heaven is. We will know everything, even the distance between heaven and hell.

The soul knows things our minds never dreamt of. Only if our soul wants our mind to know something will it make our spirit remember. Our souls know where souls really go, for how long and who and we really are. That is the knowledge the soul has over us, we have to prove we are worthy of our places. Every moment in Our lives prepares us for the next moment. Amber and Andrew wanted to know what was in the universe. How come we can't see the spirits in the air floating around us? Where do lost souls go and what do they do? All lost souls go to a purgatory planet where the spirit guides help them find the love and the light in their souls again. The spirit guides battle between the good and evil for our souls.

Andrew told Amber, "Never fight what you can't see." Never trust someone who has poison in their soul. As the poison in the soul grows so must the love in our hearts and souls grow to show them the way. Think of it as chanting a song and freedom from fear, freedom for our souls. Believing in oneself heals the mind. They learned the requirements of forgiveness, how to renew friendship, how to cherish and acknowledge each other's feelings-especially now that it had been forged during their retreat-why they had a growing-apart crisis and the intense discussion of what they meant to each other and knowing their souls were entwined. It was easy to fan the flame, like a seed that was planted in the earth and needed water to grow, they now believed in what they shared and why they stepped forward.

There comes a time when everyone has to make a choice to do the right thing. To fight one has to have hope. Having hope gives us willpower. We are all one family, yes the human species. Double whammy: when our looks fade and our eyesight fades, touch remains. Our souls have blocked from some of us what we are not supposed to know until that day when the road ends and a new turn begins. Then it'll be time to celebrate with the universe and our souls. Don't deprive yourself of what you believe in. Be a curious soul: be smack dab in the middle of it all. Don't be puffed up with pride. Take a deep breath. smell the essence of heaven and a blossoming new life while our souls step forward on the other side of the unseen world.

Chapter 10

Lavender Field

Hello, lavender field," Granny May would say when she watched her lavender blossoms swaying in the summer breeze, the heavily scented flowers she inhaled deeply to start her day. Dressed in her lavender slacks and shirt, "There are worse places I could be this morning," said Granny May, "besides this beautiful land," with a bucket full of her lavender pride. It was a Saturday morning. Her grandkids eleven-year-old Rob and ten-year-old Mark, came to visit her for the day. The boys loved their grandmother and their grandfather, who had five years ago. When Granny May felt lonely she often found peace within herself walking through her lavender field which she and her late husband Dean planted together one year before he died. Being in the field gave her pleasure and made her feel happy thinking and knowing that Grandpa Dean's spirit was around her, full of love and care, as she told her grandsons. Both loved playing in her lavender field. In her heart she was sad that Grandpa Dean died. When he fell off his horse, he died instantly. She hoped one day soon she would be with her loving Dean again. In her soul she knew better.

The creator withholds many things from us until he is ready. At that time it may not be the right thing for us and he may have something different in mind. God knows what will happen before we do, so don't strangle the Holy Spirit in your soul. Free up your spirit and yourself.

She was a very good cook. Grandpa loved her cooking, she told them, especially her pot roast. That Saturday morning Granny May forgot her roast in the oven. Something went wrong, and her house went up in a ball of fire. From the distance in her lavender field the smoke overcame her and her two grandsons Rob and Mark. Mark fainted. She picked him up in both hands, running for help, while Rob held on. "Help! Help!" A neighbor heard the call and came to their rescue.

She fell to the ground and said to her neighbor, "Pascal, please help the children!" The fire truck arrived. A fireman lifted Granny's head gently. She asked him for water. He gave her a drink of water and she took one sip while the other fire fighters contained the blaze from spreading. Granny May closed her eyes and passed on. Both grandsons checked out fine. Her house burned to ashes and her lavender field stood proudly swaying under a blanket of gray smoke in the breeze. Granny May died saving her grandsons Rob and Mark in her lavender field. Now her soul was together with Grandpa Dean, surrounded with the heavenly scent which smells like her lavender field forever.

Chapter 11

Time

Time waits on no one. What would it be like if there were no time limit, no seconds, no minutes, no hours? Would we all crumble or go about our business murmuring, much slower, with compassion, caring, understanding, sharing, forgiving, honesty, and love. Would our spirit be free? Would we stop to hear the eternal music of the universe that plays in harmony with our souls? Or notice everyone in his or her unique ways in this wonderful, beautiful, God-given universe? Would we have more awareness of the creator's presence and take a moment to pray? One must learn that the future is more important that the past, but the past shapes the future and when there's buried grief and buried sorrow, there is raw pain. We are strong enough to cry from the hollow of our souls and our broken heart.

In a timeless world would we still have hope and inspiration? How would we give the newborn lives that come into this world birthdays and remember the lives that depart from our world crossing over to the other side? Could we give them date and time when they take their last earthly breath without reconnecting with time? Is it possible? If the sun didn't have a shadow, how would the Native American tell what time it was? It would be a long way, walking a mile without time or waiting and hoping for a bus to come. It may look as if it's forever. Would you know what time of day to take your grandmother to her doctor's appointment? If time was trapped in a bottle and you found it, would you hold it to yourself, control it, or share it with the world? No one can. Only the master of heaven and earth holds time in his hands and his breath.

Time is not something that is being manufactured, designed or sold. It's free, a gift given to us. When we die it is passed on to another life in the universe whether human being or animal. Give thanks with joy and gratitude for each moment of time. With time we can do anything, tell stories, and write songs, read, built a city, heal the sick or make promises. Time is precious, time is life, time is the air we breathe; the gift of life, seconds, minutes, and hours are the time of our lives.

Chapter 12

The Soul Arrangement

Each soul and spirit are connected together wherever they are. When the time is right our souls direct us to where we should be and what we should be doing. If we pay more attention to what our souls are saying, it will direct us throughout our lives, step by step, through the life that was already chosen for us. If we try to run it will ruin us because there always be something missing inside our soul that will divide our soul and spirit. When we find that something or someone we will be completed. Every place a person has been or is going to be, our souls have been there before; every person you know, and will ever know our souls knew before; everything we do or will be doing, our souls have done before in another lifetime.

The soul is the true essence of who we are as human beings. We keep the soul we have until we die, then it be passed on to another. Others can pray for help to save our souls but we have to want to save our own souls from (evil) darkness. Every change we have gone through and will be going through, don't you know our souls have experienced it already. We may get the feeling we have done this, been there, or experienced it before. Those are the soul's signals.

This life was chosen for us before we were born. The soul made an arrangement promising the heavenly father to serve its purpose on earth and to complete our task, refraining from wrong doing while living here, which we committed in previous lives, before leaving the home base of heaven and coming to earth, then returning when our time is expired. If our tasks are not completed in the right way or something went wrong, the soul will return to home base for counseling, then be sent back to earth as another human being as many times as needed until our lesson is learned. Sometimes, in some cases, what seems like years to us is actually seconds or minutes in the spirit world. Until that soul fulfills its promise, it will repeatedly return to this world to fulfill the soul's arrangement. Then the soul becomes an angel or an archangel with a new aspect of life and new knowledge for that soul.

Maybe you have met some one for the first time and think to yourself, I know this person, but from where? You don't remember. You have met them in a former life. They are called old souls or wise souls. Have you ever done something for the first time and done it well, like painting, creating something, or fixing up a house without anyone showing you how, and you knew what to do? Believe it, you have done that before in a past lifetime. Your soul knows it and so will you.

Chapter 13

Vision

The image which stood on the rooftop looked like that of a woman dressed in a long blue sack cloth with a white veil covering her head, looking directly at me. I was only five years old and this was my first vision, to my recollection. I did not know what it was called at the time.

I was sitting on the steps of a small two-room house on a coconut, coffee, cocoa, and banana plantation estate in St. Joseph, Trinidad, West Indies, where my parents worked as laborers. It was my first home. My parents and three out of my ten siblings lived there. The kitchen was about ten feet away from the house. I saw her standing on the roof of the kitchen. I was stunned, rubbing my eyes. I pulled my hands slowly away from them then looking up again, there she stood, looking straight at me. I had my first conversion with the lady, never asking her name and don't remember if she told me it was. My innocent faith and trust in her made me feel comfortable. I was alone that sun- shiny early morning. It was the first of many occasions. Both my parents worked in the fields, so at the age of five I had to watch my younger brothers and sisters until they came home for lunch or until one of my aunts came over to take care of us.

I would be guided through strange and curious paths of life. Every time I was alone, the lady would appear, sometimes with others. She would be there in a flash. Somehow she knew when I was alone and stayed with me until someone came, then she disappeared. Physically I was always alone, but in a supernatural way I was never alone. I kept getting the feeling that I knew things before they happened or knew all my mother's secrets and her hiding places where she hid her stuff. That made my parents very angry with me. All my life no one understood. They thought that I was a very bad, crazy, little girl. There was no other explanation. That is when my life of real loneliness and heartache began, the long road of cruelty. I curled into a shell and stayed there with pain in my heart, tears in my soul, and the stain of resentment in my spirit. I had an inner anguished feeling, but a pleasant smile my face, always wanting to be good, not knowing I was good but born a little different, the wisdom within my soul gained from being reincarnated more that once. I have seen two of my past lives and knew who I was then, where I lived, and how I died.

My visions taught me how to be creative, to see the goodness in people, to be strong and kind with compassion, to be tolerant and to look toward spiritual growth. It made me become aware and understand that I was born with a spiritual gift. It gave me greater understanding, which my parents and siblings did not have at that time. My visions and dreams came from a place even deeper than my pain. God had something better in mind for me, better than I could have ever imagined, reshaping my life and creating my own self-worth, which was engraved deep into my soul. I found it with help and guidance.

Chapter 14

Spare Change

The man who is wearing the olive green winter coat, standing at the railroad tracks, is hungry. Surviving in poverty means living on spare change. See the beggars on the streets panhandling? Watch him or her, analyzing, comparing in doubt whether to hand out your spare change or not. The heartache in their hearts can be seen in their eyes.

To travel beyond the mind one has to go deep into the soul, where all the emotions are stored. Think of it as reaping a crop of grain then storing it in a safe place. First you have to open the door to get to the grains. Opening the door to the soul releases energy for spiritual growth. The soul is peace, the soul is serenity. It is comforting to the spirit, and it is giving part of ourselves.

The woman with a distant look on her face, her eyes look empty-her heart is full of fear. She may lose her home not being able to pay her bills. Where is her spare change? She has none and has nowhere to go, wondering if she will find shelter? She has no desire, not even to avoid her emotional pain, and is stuck in the moment, afraid to leap into the next moment.\

Look at the drug addict. His hand is in his pocket, looking for change so he can buy his next high, while the devil is stealing his soul and running with his mind. That poor middle-aged mother sitting on the train, she is a workaholic. What is she running from? The look on her face is a lifetime of masked pain and grief. Her smile shows happiness. Turning her head, the pain and grief slowly return. Exhaustion shows in the crows' feet around her eyes, a slight wrinkle on her face showing she is barricading her feelings from others. It is not age that is taking a toll on her but the effects of fear. Fear that she may not have enough spare change to provide for her family. Her mind is going back and forth, working overtime. Fear is disrupting her physical and emotional life. Pretending to be safe she is fatigued

but can't stop even if she is falling down. Her attention must always be occupied in order to avoid her feelings.

Children in the garbage piles are rummaging through, looking for treasure. Food is their treasure. Food that some people take for granted and throw away. When some have too much clothes, furniture, gadgets, all these things are spare change. It could help nourish and keep someone happy and healthy. It's an opportunity and a benefit to those who don't have any spare change.

What did you do with your spare change? Where did you throw it? Hey! Looking for your spare change? I've got it.

Chapter 15

Bleeding Hearts and Souls

At five years old I experienced the loss of my one-year-old sister. Her death was very confusing to me. One day she became ill and then had to be admitted to the hospital for a few weeks. The next thing I knew she was dead, but I had no idea what dying meant. When my parents brought her body home for viewing, I saw my sister's lifeless body laying in the coffin, her eyes wide open. How could she be dead with her eyes wide open? Every movement I made, I thought she was watching me, but I was told that she was dead and that my brothers and my sisters and myself were never going to see her again. She was in heaven. It made my heart bleed like a wounded, frightened, wild animal and my soul like a raging river.

My life and my soul were tormented. That was in the year 1958. From that day on I had to walk past the cemetery where she was buried on my way to school. There was no way to avoid the cemetery. The school was on the boundary with the cemetery. I cried every day sitting in my classroom, which overlooked the almond tree my sister was buried under. For one year the tears came pouring down my face. I then became accustomed to the painful situation in my life.

From the time I first knew what a bleeding heart and soul felt like there has always been one incident after another, on and on, again and again, back and forth. The blood flows from my heart, engulfing every fiber of my being like a fountain. When one problem has solved I would find myself thinking, when will the other shoe drop. I waited to hear the familiar sound of that emotional roller coaster for almost forty-nine years.

I didn't wake up one morning and suddenly find that my soul was finally free. I worked at it for many tiresome years, sometimes almost giving up, but then something would happen and make me want to work even harder. At a crucial moment on Sunday morning, February 10, 2002 5:30 A.M., I found freedom for my bleeding heart and soul. My spirit felt light from the inside of my body to the outside. Floating on the wings of spiritual love. For the first time in my lifetime nothing was that important to me that couldn't wait.

My past was a distant memory and the future would bring new experiences. What was happening at the present moment and circumstance was all that mattered, the experience of freeing my soul. Now my life was free and I knew that I about to live my best life ever. There was nothing that could trigger any excruciatingly painful emotional memory from the past. This was my moment and this was the present. If one waits, when the time is right, the door will opened if you don't walk away before you hear the knock. By knocking anyone can gain freedom from a bleeding heart and soul. I am not saying that my heart and soul will never bleed again, but in ways that will not contaminate my life. As long as we live in this world we will experience a bleeding heart and soul, each and every one of us. That is the most painful path to life.

For me that freedom did not come without a price. Imprisonment and the captivity of my soul isolated my spirit, which fed on my energy my whole life. When one's soul is free one's spirit can fly. I believe that the soul is like a mirror. You have to look into the mirror. The longer you look and the harder you look, the more you will see. The soul is like that; eventually you see what you need. The freedom and healing of my bleeding heart and soul was appropriate for me at the appropriate time in my life. Now it tastes like honey. Now I can live. I can live life.

Chapter 16

Tailspin

The bus operator frequently talks as if his life is in a tailspin (meaning when things get out of control, fear consumes our minds, and we have to look into our souls to find out what is real). He talks about his overweight wife, the way she looks, and the smell of her bad body odor to the passengers on the 5 P.M. city bus. He always has an attitude; the slightest thing ticks him off. At first impression he looks like a clam and easygoing guy but under the surface lies a river of anger that runs into the sea. Like the current that is beneath the deep surface, anyone stepping into the water will not know there is an undercurrent. By then it may be too late.

Some tailspins can lead to imminent destruction and unlimited grief. The massacre on September 11, 2001, will forever be engraved in our minds, hearts, and souls. It will live in our spirits in this lifetime and beyond. The thousands of lives went up into flames or were buried in a watery grave. From flames of fire to a river of water. Oh? How sad and tearful the universe felt, as angels floated down from heaven with wings as big and strong as an eagle. Heaven's gates opened up on 9/11. The beam of white light shone on the United States of America. The angel's voices were one while they slowly circled and hovered around the World Trade Centers in New York City, sending out signals to the souls of the victims in the universe that something bad was about to happen, showing and leading them down the path they were supposed to have taken.

That day life was in a tailspin here in America. There were fear and panic everywhere one turned. Every eye one looked into was full of pain and tremendous fear as they watched the two airplanes hit the towers. Feelings of fear, anger, anxiety, and despair overwhelmed everyone in America and the world. Everyone who was alive felt their stomachs churn with thousands of butterflies fluttering with emotions, dancing with a bad feeling that our lives were about to in a tailspin and it was up to us to do something to stop the pain. All kinds of fearful thoughts and possibilities ran through the minds or every living and dying human being who was witnessing or experiencing the horrendous destruction of the twin towers in this strikingly beautiful, jaw-dropping city.

September 11, 2001, when the attack on America happened, was a day of the most intense fear I had ever experienced in my life because we have seen the same scenario on the television news, in the movies, even read about war in the newspaper, but to know it's real, here and now. Still in doubt, it felt as if the northeast wind knocked the breath out of me. I landed on my knees and shouted out, "O my God, please save the people inside the towers! Save New York City! Save America, even the world! Please forgive us all our sins."

As we watched the mass destruction unfolding on TV, the World Trade Center towers came crumbling down, lights went out, phones lines went down, and the light in our life went out at that moment. The sound of sirens with flashing lights from the New York Fire Department, New York Police Department, and emergency medical technicians everywhere. People were running in every direction, scrambling for cover, not knowing where to go. There was nowhere to go, nowhere to run, nowhere to hide. Screaming and crying filled the air. Men, women, and children were covered with white dust. This was doomsday in New York City. Fire was everywhere. People were flying through windows from the towers like Superman while others ran back and forth in confusion. Debris came pouring down like a rainstorm. Gray plumes of smoke filled the skies of Manhattan. Everything was covered with dust. New York City was in lockdown, no one going in or out.

All the heavenly angels' arms were outstretched, hand in hand, wings outstretched, each wing tip touching each other as the angels descended upon New York City, Ground Zero, Washington, and also Pennsylvania in silence. Into a circle of white light unconditional love, embracing the city and America, shielding her with the armor of love and protection, the angels were very busy helping those who were resisting crossing over. That day when New York City went into a tailspin, the angels helped the New York firefighters; the New York police officers; the Port Authority officers; the hospitals; the doctors, nurses, and medical personnel; the E.M.Ts, and all those who were chosen by a higher power to serve in this crisis.

All different languages were heard telling the story about how the planes crashed into the World Trade Towers. Father Judd, our earth angel, lost his life while helping N.Y. firefighters. They carried his body down the street and laid him in front of the altar. He is now an angel in heaven, comforting the thousands of souls who died.

On 9/11 everyone walked in the shadow of death. When it was over, Ground Zero looked like the gateway to hell and the valley of death in New York City. The universe brought them all together. There was no color, race, nationality, or status lines; it was as if time had stood still. In slow motion every soul, every heart beat. Every voice, dead or alive, became one; everyone felt the same pain. In fear and hopelessness, we were all one family in the universe on 9/11. survived and who died was their destiny. It may sound cold but from everything bad that happens something good comes from it. We have more compassion for others; we are more focused on observing and cleansing the world of possible manmade destruction so others may know what freedom means and feels like in the U.S.A., for she is the leader of the world and an example for peace and freedom. She's not perfect but she carries the weight of the world and the needs of the people. She showed strength, power, bravery, fearlessness, even kindness, love, and understanding when needed. She is my homeland, yours and anyone who needs freedom in life. She is the mother who wept for her birth children, her adopted children, and the children of the world. Every September 11, the universe mourns. The world went into a tailspin and the past interlocked with the future forever, but most of all she is still standing. She is America the bravest, America the strongest, where heroes are made and angels will fly.

Chapter 17

Bread Basket

His mean streak made him grunt out to the pastor, "You have food to eat and clothes to wear. Don't forget to lie, to cry, and to die." The homeless man was having a meltdown. The only home he had for the past eight years was a cardboard box at the side entrance of the subway station on Utica Avenue in Brooklyn. An old shopping cart someone must have thrown away was filled with raggedy clothes, empty soda bottles, a can of expired black beans he found in the trash, a sandwich wrapped in plastic wrap someone gave him yesterday, and a couple of beer cans, all his possessions.

The clothes he wore smelled, as did his breath. His hands black with layers of dirt.

Even his fingernails one wonder when the last time he had a bath and clean undergarments. On his feet he wore a pair of mismatched shoes he found somewhere.

Stumbling as he walked, no one knew his name nor did they bother to ask. The homeless man entered the church one Sunday morning as the pastor preached about having one breadbasket filled with a variety of things. Then lo and behold, the man shouted, "My name is Jake." He pointed at the pastor. "Here is my bread basket," reaching into his pants pocket, which he held up with two pieces of string, and pulled out a small tin can. "This is my breadbasket, see?" He turned the empty can upside down. He said to the pastor standing at the altar, "Why don't you fill my basket? Better, yet fill it with some bread, some honey, some money, and a place to sleep. My family abandoned me twelve years ago. I lost my job, my house, my money, and my car and I ended up living in the streets like a dog." The congregation looked up at Jake, some whispering among themselves. The homeless man's taunting gaze made some of the congregation feel somewhat uncomfortable.

The pastor stepped down from the pulpit, his hand reaching out to Jake. "My brother, you have come to the right place. It doesn't matter why you lost everything, what matters now is that you are here in the house of God and no one is homeless or hungry here."

Jake answered, "I'm hallucinating," and placed his hand into Pastor Rafe's hand. "Okay, no more chitchatting and bellyaching," replied Pastor Rafe. "Please have a seat and at the end of service one of the sisters will take care of you."

Jake ignored the pastor said about no chitchattin. "So you really mean someone will take care of me?" thumping his chest with both hands, at the corner of his eyes tears rolled down his dirty unshaved face. "How I longed to hear those words.

"The universe has brought you home, Jake," said Sister Karen. "Close your eyes. What do you see?"

"Nothing," answered Jake.

"Open your eyes. Tell me, what do you see?"

"People?" answered Jake.

"No," Karen said. "Look, your breadbasket is filled with a variety of things. Yes, you have outward strength, inner strength, inner love in your soul to strengthen your spirit. See you also have now the physical things to strengthen your body, fruits, food, and plenty of it. Having half a loaf and sharing it with someone who is less fortunate, giving it whole heartedly in return, down the road you will receive a whole loaf from that half loaf and your breadbasket will always be full."

"Oh! I see what you mean." Shaking his head, Jake smiled. External fruits what are now and everlasting food is beyond and that is indefinite.

Chapter 18

Finish Line

"Foot dragging is not the way to go about life."

"Aren't we picky today?"

"Dave, you're in that nasty mood again."

Susie looked at Dave with disgust. "You know, Annie," Susie said to her friend, "He never gives me feelings of satisfaction, not even self-worth, only pain and rejection. There is no real connection with Dave. I never belonged here, Annie. I feel shame burning up and down my spine and my heart. His thoughtless actions and shameful lies make it impossible to focus on what I want out of life. "With a sense of hostility, Susie's face went stone cold.

When Dave Shepard met Susie Carter five years ago, Susie thought Dave would definitely be her knight in shining armor. Both vowed to stay together forever, no matter what was going on in their lives.

Annie interrupted, "You both started a race, to a love race, get to the finish line. Remember that kind of race doesn't run smooth. You have to hold on to your sanity and the love, respect, and trust you have for each other."

"Are you conspiring against me?" Susie said to Annie. Tension started to build up between the two women. "Let's not get carried away now. I'm still deeply in love with Dave."

Susie ran off to the powder room, leaving Dave and Annie sitting at the restaurant table, sipping red wine. Susie came back a few moments later, leaned over to Dave, and said, "I need to breathe. Do you mind?"

"No" Dave said. "Take as much time as you need."

Annie stood up. "Do you need company?" "Thanks, but this is something I have to do alone."

Looking at the water from a small restaurant in Long Island, Susie decided to go down to the shore for a walk. She took off her boots, stepped into the cold water, and looked up at the rain cloud that was about to burst any minute. This is great. It's almost springtime. The trees have started budding, birds are on the swaying branches chirping, some flying from branch to branch picking at their feathers, others wiping their beaks on the branches and flying from tree top to tree top. That big old oak tree will be full of green leaves shading us from the warm sunlight.

Soon the lilac and honeysuckle will bloom and its scented fragrance will fill the spring air. The beautiful cherry blossoms will be everywhere. Everyone will peel off their winter garments and overcoats. Love will be in the air-young love, old love, renewed love, love everywhere, in the street and in the parks. Laughter will be in the air, laughter everywhere. Sweet music will fill our ears and linger on in our minds. Old folks strolling hand in hand; children riding bikes and scooters on the sidewalks, weaving among the shoppers; shopping bags banging on our sides as we walk pass the crowd. "Excuse me, I'm coming through, I'm sorry. "Smiles here and there, others tuning around and making a face or rolling an eye, giving the finger or "talk to the hand" sign. Hurrying along to catch a bus, running down the subway steps to catch a downtown or uptown train, hailing a taxi, or hitching a ride with a friend to get home anxiously.

Dave tapped Susie on her shoulder as she walked on the beach, drawing lines in the sand, remembering why she fell in love with him. The cool end of the winter breeze passing on her face felt good. She took a long deep breath and slowly exhaled. Dave said, "Susie, I know what I have to do continue this race." They both looked into each other's eyes and deep into each other's soul. Back at the restaurant the dinner crowd cheered and the band played louder as Dave and Susie walked back to their table where Annie waited. "I'm very happy for you guys." Before they could sit she started to say, "Let this be a lesson. Spring is the rebirth. It's the rebirth of love, relationships, and for you two." Coming from her it was comforting for both Dave and Susie.

In life, when you stumble and fall and you pick yourself up the crowd will see you are determined to reach the finish line and they will cheer you on. The energy from them will give you the strength, courage, and willpower to help you reach the finish line. Winning is not always important but finishing the race that is what counts. I know you all can make it and do what you were meant to do in this lifetime. The journey to the destination is what pushes one, the thrill, the excitement, and the music on the way. As the north wind on the symphony of music plays, you'll keep pushing. Eventually you will come to the finish line with a feeling of joy, triumph, and completion in your soul. That is only if you can find the magic within your souls.

Chapter 19

Nesting Place

At the doctor's office in walked young and old people, some with screaming, crying babies; old folks reminiscing about their past with joy. One can see their eyes light up. Black, brown, blue, and green eyes all light up with the same pride, while others go dim when talking about bad past experiences. Some with canes, walkers, wheelchairs, going by with cramped hands, shaking, complaining about their aches, cramps, and chronic pains. They all nest at the doctor's office, hoping they will feel better after their visit and also leave making a new friend.

People nest on lines at the banks and supermarkets. Some chew gum, some talk a lot, others make new friends complaining about their teenagers. Some count their money mentally, others physically, while some get impatient with the bank tellers or the checkout person at the supermarket, saying they are too slow.

At the movies all the seats are filled with nesting people, black, white, red, brown, or in between, some up under someone's arms, others with popcorn in one hand, soda between their knees or on the floor, people shuffling from one seat to another. Human beings nest. Like birds we flock together. We don't build our nest in such a way that when it rains, snows, or there is a windstorm, our nest gets wet or easily blown away. At home most of us feel safe from the rest of the world. No one wants to be caged up like a darn animal in a zoo looking through wire netting.

"I want to find my nesting place too," said Allan to his father Joe. "I'm eighteen and I can do what I want."

His father said, "You bastard, so you want to have your nesting place?" with a very angry voice, shouting so loud that someone could hear him three doors down. "Okay, Allen, you delusional, foolish boy." Joe chuckled. "Where will you go? What will you do? How will you take care of yourself?" asked his father. "You're dropping out of high school. All you do is lay around the house doing nothing all day or talk on the phone like a girl or go out at night doing hell knows what!"

"Oh shut up, Dad, you are the one who told me to be a man," sticking his finger in Joe's face. All of Allen's anger focused toward his father, the boy walking around and around the kitchen table.

Joe took one step back. "Allen, have you any direction behind this, any positive plans?" Pounding on the kitchen table, he said, "Where is my boy?"

Allen answered, "I'm not a boy any more. You listen up, Dad, I'm a man, a man, Dad. Look at me, I'm a man standing in front of you and you can't see that." Joe pulled out a chair and slumped down, his hands covering his face for a minute, then realizing for the first time his son stood up to him not as a boy but as a young man who needed to go out into the world to find his nesting place.

Walking away, "I'm sorry, Dad," Allen said to his father. "You may not understand it but it's my decision to make. It's in my soul, I can feel it in my spirit It's time to let go."

Joe, a single parent, took care of his son when his wife Dee-Dee died. His son's words kept repeating in his head, I'm not a boy, I'm a man, Dad. Joe was left with more questions in his soul than the pain and fear in his heart for his son who was taking a new direction in his life. Sweating, sitting at the kitchen table, speechless, looking out the window as he watched his son drive away then fade in the distance, his soul cried out, Good luck, take care, goodbye, my son.

Chapter 20

A Child Prays

Lucy Graham, a scrawny little country girl, loved the outdoor life but she carried a secret in her heart from her friends. In fact her brothers and sisters also knew about the family secrets. They lived on a farm way out in the countryside in North Carolina and had to work very hard, waking up at the crack of dawn to tend to the animals. Little Lucy worried about her parents day in and day out. Any suspicious look on their faces or the sense of bitterness in their voices clamped at her heart with panic, devouring her innocence and childhood. That made her live in a fantasy world but in reality her parents had fallen out of love with each other and decided to stay together for the children's sake. They lived with a lot of humiliation; sometimes they went berserk among themselves. When their parents had fights, Wendi, the children's mother, would leave for months while Mike, their father, had to take care of three small boys and girls under the age of twelve. The children, bless their hearts, had to be shuffled from one family member to another, back and forth, day after day, with their belongings packed up in a brown paper bag, walking around like alley cats.

Lucy, the first born, had to carry the burden. It made her weak to the bones. She would zone out at times. Both parents manipulated the children into choosing sides. When they chose to be with Mike, Wendi said, "Hell no." She inflicted pain on them by burning their fingers on the stove or by making them kneel on a rood grater one-foot long by six inches wide for half an hour with no small rocks in each hand outstretched. That's how Wendi's mother Ruth had punished her as a little girl when she misbehaved. There would be imprints or grater marks with blood running down their knees, like the imprints of a former life on one's soul. When they chose Wendi's side, Mike would curse at them, sometimes even chasing them away from home. "No, Papa, please don't make us leave! We love you,

Papa." He would make the children kneel, whipping them unmercifully until they cried out, "I can't take any more!" There was no way to escape or avoid the conflict in their lives.

When the family got back together things went well for a while, then back to the same old ways. After some lime passed it became predictable to Lucy and she was always choked up with tears. Every time her parents raised their voices the children thought they were to blame. When the other children praying, "Gentle Jesus, meek and mild, look upon this little child, "Lucy was praying:

Dear God help us remain as a family together.

Please make Mama and Papa stop fighting with each another.

I'm afraid that one day my father might kill my mother.

I'm so tired of having to get in the middle every time they fight to protect Mama.

Please God, make them stop cursing and screaming at each other.

I'm afraid to sleep at night, I might miss when they start fighting and one of them might get hurt and we'll be left alone. What will I do?

Who will comb our hair and feed us? Who will take care of us we get sick?

I'm so afraid to breathe loud when I'm listening in case my parents start fighting.

God, I tremble when I tiptoe to check on Mama and Papa to know if they are still alive.

Please God, make me well so I can go home again to protect Mama from Papa.

I'm so afraid if I die Mama will be scared of Papa.

Bless my mother and father and my brothers and sisters.

Please bless all the little children who are afraid tonight.

Amen!

Eleven-year-old Lucy became very sick. She had kidney problems and only had twenty-four hours to live. Her shyness made her vulnerable, knowing if she died she would not be there for her parents. Lucy fought tooth and nail to stay alive. She had a very strong willpower of her own and the need to protect her family. Six weeks staying in the hospital, and Lucy's father never came to visit her, not even once. Maybe she did not mean anything to her father or was too much trouble, she thought, her sad lonely eyes questioning her mother. Her heart fell like a forest that was on fire, burning with pain faster and faster, trampling her spirit without blinking. She waited for the mother's answer. First Wendi embraced her, then gave her daughter the same answer. "Honey, your father is working hard and can't get away now, Lucy!"

"Why won't he come, why?"

When visiting hours were over Lucy would pull covers over her head and cry her eyes out. She never knew the truth of why her father never came to visit her. She prayed the same prayer every night, then one night when Lucy prayed she saw Jesus on the Cross. To her amazement in her vision his chest opened up and out came a white drove, which spoke to her. "When your human strength has come to its weakest your spirit will rise and you will no longer be the forgotten lost sheep. This life will be just a memory, a memory it will be and the more you walk a path when the time comes you will know which is the right path."

Wednesday, the day of her discharge from the hospital, Lucy looked one more time for her father to come. "Mama, did you come alone?"

"Yes," answered her mother.

Lucy shouted, "There isn't going be a next time! I'm sick of listening to you saying Papa has to work. I don't want to hear it anymore,"

Lucy left the country life behind. She is a fashion designer and lives in Chicago with her own family. She found the path that was right for her.

The essence of the human body is the soul, without the soul, the body can't exist. Human emotions come from the soul. It's then transferred to the heart and intertwined with our personality. Most people walk around as wolves in sheep's clothing. When they get behind closed doors the wool jacket is pulled off then the real person shows themselves. For Lucy she wore the sheep's clothing and never had to pull it out because she was true in her soul.

One of my experiences is similar to Lucy's. When I was a young girl I took a look at my family and got the feeling I didn't belong. This is not my family, this isn't who I am, this is not even my body. Tugging and biting on my arms in tears, This is not me. I didn't understand as a teenager, even as a young woman. I kept having the same uncomfortable feeling that something deep in my soul was unknown to me. I am now a middle-aged woman and I still have the same thoughts and action, which have plagued me for almost all my life. One day I looked at the bathroom mirror, asking questions which taunted me so much. Who am I? What am I? Why am I here? And where did I come from?

Like the white dove that spoke to Lucy, the image of a woman I had never seen in my life was looking right at me. From where she stood, the garment she wore, my soul recognized. Aha! The image in the mirror was me. One soul, two different bodies, in different time zones revealed who, what, where, and why. The soul is like the open sea way beyond the horizon, collecting information and pulling out knowledge it has stored for centuries. It hides nothing and everything has to be purged out. The spirit sails throughout this universe like a boat on high seas. Both the soul and the spirit store information for the next reincarnation. Wisdom in the world is the soul and spirit's own time capsule.

If one feels lost within one's self, learn to ask questions. You have the right to know, to find your own path in your inner child. Pray and you will find the answers in your soul. The soul and the spirit go together just like hands and gloves in the height of winter to keep our hands warm, protecting them from frostbite. soul and spirit can't be separated for long. They need each other. The spirit makes us witty and guides us but it can be separated from the body. Leaving it behind, the spirit shines. It is the orb that makes us glow and enlightens our hearts with inspiration. The soul shows us the past, present, and future, also allowing the truth to be known, making us who we are. It is important for us to believe in God, essentially striving for good and fulfillment.

When one's soul is fully awakened the eyes are open and the wisdom from the soul is known. The eyes are connected to the soul. As the mother and her two small children were swimming in the sea, suddenly a raging current pulled one of her children. The mother was holding on tight to her child's right foot, the raging current then fed on both, pulling and sucking them further and further into the ocean. She didn't want to let go of her child because her child was a part of her. Without her child she might as well be asleep, with the child she can pass down her wisdom and knowledge. What is in the heart and soul comes out into the reality of life, the soul's rites of passage.

Chapter 21

Stuck In The Middle

A heart that has been bruised, knocked around, and battered all her life, she has felt it in her gut, throughout her soul and her physical form. No one take away the emotional pain in her heart, which pumps blood flowing with the pain of her life suffering. She wanted the desire to remove the pain and the loneliness and to connect in a real relationship from the get go.

Beth Singer was the estranged wife of Marshal. He drank a lot and while coming home from one of his drinking sprees, saw his wife sound asleep on his side of the bed. He became very furious and dragged her out by her hair, kicking her upside the head, staggering as a drunken fool does, goading her on, then transforming himself into some kind of a monster, roaring like a lion. Beth away into a corner. Marshal came at her in a rage. Covering her face while peeking through her fingers, Marshal got closer and closer, yelling, "I'll drink you up like chicken soup, fly you like French fries, flip you over like a double cheeseburger, then toss you up like a tossed salad. Woman, you got that!" With horns coming out of his head and foaming at the mouth, he kept jumping around like a kangaroo.

Beth's weight kept her from being able to move fast, cushioning herself between the bed and the dresser with her hands on her hips. "Excuse me! Hello? Is that what you are doing, punishing yourself? Out of control, walking in here drunk and stinking like a skunk." Her luscious lips were swollen when he punched her in the mouth. Marshal said to Beth, "You want to leave, you know your way to the door. Stop talking and get out." She started to say something. "I don't want to hear it," he said, "don't you make a mistake and sleep on my side of the bed again." Later on, his beast-like features slowly started to disappear when he looked at her lying on the bed in the guestroom asleep, he was a very mean man. Marshal sneaked into the closet, waited until it was dark and everyone was asleep, came out, and stood at the side of the bed. He looked at his wife, then pinned her down and started banging her head, each time harder than the time before. Like a drum it echoed in her ears. While trying to pull herself up, he would slap her in the face. She had to remind herself of the lifetime of pain and exhaustion she had suffered. The damage and the deep emotional wounds she sustained. No one said you have to be tolerant and persevere this monstrously abusive behavior. As the minutes slipped away she mentioned her firm faith. He laughed aloud and spit on her. Sometimes the closer you get to what you want the more you feel as if you're slipping from its grasp. She then crawled onto the floor on her hands and knees.

She couldn't go back to fix it and she couldn't go forward because she was stuck in the middle and was afraid of her yesterday, today, and tomorrow. The unbearable grief and strife went on. Walking on the edge of her fear, inside of her she knew something was lacking.

Beth always wandered deep into the woods when she had problems, for hours she would sit under an old pine tree. On this day she saw a small golden box, very unusual looking, glittering under some dried leaves next to her. A of light bust out from behind the pine tree, slowly moving from behind one tree to another, disappearing before she could wink, then standing still as she approached and grasped the golden box.

Opening the box slowly and peeking inside she saw a pair of clear contact lenses. A voice came from behind her left shoulder. "They are mystical eyes. Put them on, Beth.

"How do you know my name?" she asked.

"I know everything about you. Don't be afraid, put them on. They can only be worn with a good heart and good intentions."

When she put on the pair of mystical eyes Beth saw everyone's thoughts, what they were thinking, what they felt, where they were going, their illnesses, their pains, their plans good or bad, every twinge, every movement and the next. Beth saw the past, present, and future.

The voice said, "Cleanse your thoughts and you will see the real mystical world the way it should have been."

She was sick and tired of being everyone's poster child for tragedy. Having the mystical eyes made her feel important, she could see every element in a person's body, every disease in their blood, sweat, and tears. The remedy would appear next to the person. The mystical eyes showed her herbal healing. Word spread like wild-fire. People from all over the world came by hundreds. They even brought their animals, but only those who had faith were healed. Those who were skeptical, their disease became blue for everyone to see, what disease they had on the inside showed up on the outside of their bodies in a blue patch.

People send out two kind of messages, one verbal, the other is what you don't hear. Why wasn't this said or that? Some of the people who were there for healing lied convincingly about their illnesses. They knew the difference between good and evil and knew what was wise and what was not but chose the music of a lie and did not know that it would come back to haunt them. Not everyone came with good intentions. Some were deceptive.

Marshal was very deceptive. He came dressed in a disguise among the gathering to see what his wife was really doing. When he saw what Beth did he became jealous and planned to steal the golden box with the pair of contact lenses and use them for his own purposes. Beth was told she was never to use them for her own purposes, that it would turn to the dark side, that it was meant to be shared with the world.

One evening Marshal followed her, watching her every move. She knew his every intention. When she got home she took off the mystical eyes. Only when Beth put the lenses on did they became mystical eyes. Putting them back into the box, she forgot to close the box. When it was closed only Beth could open the box. Marshal decided to make his move. It was late April, a gray, somber, spring day. The sky was cloudy and the sound of loud, cracking thunder rolled one after the next. Bright lightning flashed. It made one feel as if the world was going to end. The sky opened up raining heavily, water gushing from the streets into the sewers. There was no one on the streets, just parked cars with raindrops rolling off the hoods. A clash with thunder and lightning made a few parked car alarms go off. The flowers of the lilac tree branches became heavy from the rain. Dried branches fell on the sidewalk from the oak tree.

Marshal stole the pair of clear contact lenses, went down to the cellar, put them on, got into his car, and drove off. On his way he saw his past and his present but could not see his future. He lashed out by cursing with vengeance. His car swayed from side to side and he could not recognize where he was and what was happening to him, but relaxed when he took a drink, then another and another.

He saw beautiful rooms. What blazes was that? Entering one of the many rooms there were treasures from the floor to the ceiling: gold, diamonds, rubies, emeralds, and pearls. He was excited. "This is a once in a lifetime chance and it's all mine." When he reached for the treasure he saw a seven-headed serpent coming at him hissing. One head said, "I have been waiting for you. Come in." Behind him there were horses galloping. He could not move. There were also swords fighting, blades with no one holding them. Close to his face Marshal heard voices talking to him. A voice in his head said, You should not have done that. He spun around almost falling.

"What?" Marshal said.

The voice said, Stole the contact lenses, and for a minute he knew that he was in his car and felt a hand pushing him out of his car. Turning around there was no one for miles, he began to run toward the hills. The more he ran the faster his natural eyesight faded, until he couldn't see ever again and went insane. He could not find his life or his way back. By using the mystical eyes with bad intentions the evil within his soul come to life and he was trapped in his fear. Loneliness feeds on loneliness like bees feed on pollen from flowers, it devours the spirit. Beth's hurt and loneliness was finally gone because she was not stuck in the middle any more.

Chapter 22

Let Your Love Shine

Susan Mills wanted more love and help in her life and pleaded for God's help. "Right now I have zero tolerance and forgiveness and I'm tried of waiting for help to come and I am very angry. What am I doing wrong to cause this crisis in my life? Whether it is my intentions or not, why do I feel like a scapegoat? How weak am I as a human being in my soul? You understand better than I do these actions of mine. I'm admitting to all my terrible mistakes and all the wrongdoing." She wanted God to help her destroy the wall she had put up to protect her, no argument here with you, God.

Susan pleaded not only for herself but also on behalf of everyone in this world to let his love shine on them and on her. "We need your love for everyone to see. Let it shine in the heart of the child in tears, the newborn babies. We want it to shine on the men and women who are sitting in jail, shine in the soul of a killer, the heart of a thief, shine for the world to see high above in the sky. your love shine for peace, let it shine, shine in the Middle East.

"On the trigger, Lord, of the soldier's gun, let your love shine in his heart. On the hungry child, the angry man, in the sorrowful mother for her lost child. Let it shine on the fatherless or motherless children. That is a good reason. Please let your love shine in the homeless lives, in the poor man's heart and the troubled and lonely hearts for this world to see. Lord, in the darkness of this world and the darkest heart and the dying man's eyes, let it shine for him to see. Shine in the big guy's aching heart, in the tears that flow, shine in his eyes for the world to see. Let your love shine on the river in the valley below and the mountain tops, in the breeze that blows. Shine here on earth in the breath that we breathe. Put your love in every heart that hates, let it shine on the terrorist in his heart. Open his eyes and let your love shine in his angry heart flowing far and wide for the world to see. You know

that this world needs your love to shine and that is the reason why we need your blessing for love so much. Shine on the dying man's heart for all to see in their last breath of worldly life and that's one more reason to let your love shine like the sun and moon in the sky, like the stars that shine for the world to see."

We are living on borrowed time in a rented body, when our time is up and this body's lease is expired there may be no lease renewal for us. God was fed up with us fighting with one another and on this day that Susan Mills prayed for help, he put a stop to this world's madness by sending a great earthquake for a day to all the lands and countries of the world. No one was spared, he had to teach us a lesson in love for this world. In her dream all the mountains exploded, the seas raised high, almost touching the lowest cloud in the sky. The earth opened up in every corner of the world, simultaneously gobbling up everyone and everything. There was no one alive, no trees standing. The opening in the earth swallowed up all and the seas seeped slowly into the cracks of the earth. It lasted for days, no one had time to say goodbye, not even to say a prayer. He had to show us that we didn't have to pray because of the lack of peace and love. It was always there with us and all we had to do was look around.

There were ghost-like forms of non-existent human bodies floating, walking through each other, seeing, hearing, and reading each thought of ghost energy moving in the air. Everything we did before our world ended spirits and ghost did the same things, in the same places, taking care of others, giving birth, going to the malls. Ghost life took over. Our swimming, dancing, crying, and laughter went on, living as ghosts in a ghost world.

All the gods and supernatural holy beings watched as some of the bad and evil gods and beings of the lower dimensions were send back to witness what influence and destruction they had left behind. When the world was young before God ended it because of greed, lust, and their greediness for earthy powers, they couldn't see the love that shone in their hearts and souls.

Meanwhile as the world was ending, some saw their demons and the evil in their hearts, others saw the love that shone. What we had in our souls we all saw on that one day which was the longest day in the ghost world. We all begged and humbled for God to end this day. Not until everyone believed at the end of the day and saw the love that shone before us. All the gods saw the love that shined before they destroyed the world in their time and promised to use their powers for good. Today their spirits roam the earth, manifesting in some human beings, doing the same thing they did in ancient times. The gods and supernatural beings of ancient times walk the earth. The evil ones abuse their by seeking material things. They were rebellious and indecent; their twisted minds caused them to provoke the people to worship them. God Almighty had to banish them from walking this earth, scattering their spirits to the four corners of the universe, knowing that they could never walk this earth in their human flesh again.

God began to change the world back to the way it was before he ended it. Some of the gods were sent back to their homes. While the gods and beings of the lower dimensions had to let his love shine among themselves. Finally every one saw his love that shines in the world.

He rewards us with a peaceful life in this world, letting his love shine in each and everyone of us. We were never again afraid of listening to the music in the background coming from our souls; each soul has enough love to shine for a lifetime. So why can't we see that? Maybe we don't recognize it because we are not sensitive enough to the soul and are not listening. Maybe we have to take wrong turns in life to see the love that shines in our soul at the very last moment to make us believers. Instead of masquerading we should listen to our inner self, to learn the true stories of our souls. What secrets of the ancient world we need to know to make this a peaceful world, there is only one divine power, One God. He unleashes plagues into the world for a purpose, to consume the stubbornness, arrogance, and unbelief. The world vomits out its evil. Therefore we must cherish the gift that he has given to us for a time. It will be taken away someday.

This earth is full of God's knowledge and mystical mysteries. When the old order of ways has passed away then the new will begin, for everything turns in time. The world itself will forever live on. Only the life forms and the things in this world will perish, then a new life will begin, which will be a New World. We can change this world's future by letting his love shine. The closer we come to that victory the more we will be tested along the way and the harder it will become. The gods and holy beings are the watchmen of the world. So we need to respect what the universe is saying. It shouldn't be blown off. It can soften our hearts or torture our souls and spirits.

It is clear that something has to be done about the eye-balling anger and hatred that possesses the world. Everyone wants the joy of being alive but turns it into refried beans of the ancient times. We are like parade mongers of this world demonstrating for peace and love, passing from zone to zone, when all we have to do is let his love shine for all to see. Moving away from the old ways we can learn better ways instead of being scorpions among ourselves and being astonished when thing go bad. God is never too busy to help us. Maybe this is his way of disciplining us, or it's procedural change to let his love shine in the world in an effective way. No one is above him.

Chapter 23

Mind Games

When your soul is eye-balling and screaming at you, what do you do? Turn away, walk around thinking in the cloud and can't see in front of you, burying your head in the water as a pelican searching for fish. Stuck with the eye-balling, playing musical chairs in your mind, thinking there is no up side to this—mind games. Will this be a showdown? Dumb idea, trying to determine what to achieve.

When your soul is screaming at you what do you say? "No, no! Chill out, kid. Don't you ever cross me now, hey!" What if the soul wants to rat you out, unleashing the true you, opening up the gates of your own hell, and in return you get everything you deserved with an impact, escalating between the soul and the mind. Oh, no! Here it comes! Make some friends and fewer enemies. That way we didn't waste time in other areas spouting off about our foolish mind games. Quivering with delight while our mind games may skyrocket with others. Some feel as a wall and a ball bouncing back and forth of the wall and while you're shuffling along, kicking up dust in someone's face. Yeah, you low-life piece of crap, moron.

The haggard-looking man enjoys playing mind games with his friend, shaking his head, which made her react with anger. Don't you make promises you could never keep. Her mouth flows like a waterfall nothing stays. Her boyfriend promised to take her to Hawaii for a vacation but changed his mind two days before the trip. Tension began quickly. You don't appreciate me. Her words strongly pushed from her soul. "This is not working this is not a wish from a fountain or from a wishing well, a dream or a myth. It's real. Do you see a sign on my forehead saying I'm stupid? You took a step forward and two steps back for whatever reason.

"This is absolutely absurd. This has to stop, I'm not a loony toon who popped out of a loony bin or a loose cannon. We have been growing apart for some time and I'm acknowledging that, so please quit with the mind games. It's over. I have been feeling it deep in my soul each day, more and more, even in the marrow in my bones. You have made me feel like a lost cause. It's over. Don't give yourself any grief. Good bye.?

The bridge between our mind, heart, soul, and spirit is always connected in our thoughts. It is always fighting to show us what's right. Mind games began with Adam and Eve and the forbidden fruit centuries ago. The gods who were mean played mind games with the peasants when the world was young. Today we all play some kind of mind games at times. Sometimes it is difficult to accept people as who they really are but when this life has ended the soul will always remember us even if no one else will. We all need a shakedown at times to remind us why we are here. Call it an aftermath soul reminder. Mind games are toxic to the heart and soul. It's a mind full of poisons. We should not be surprised or disappointed when some people profit by slicing pieces of everything along the way. Others get crushed as speed dumps and most give back what they got passing through the many potholes of the players who play the mind games. Too often we hear stories about disruption of lives, people who intentionally hurt others. Mind games aren't always harmless. It can be very destructive and may destroy relationships, families, and friendships, even nations, brothers, sisters, and parents, pitting them against each other. Most dangerous is the one that deceives the heart.

For instance, a young couple was scheduled to get married one Sunday afternoon in June. The ceremony was to take place at a small chapel on the West Side, followed by a horse and carriage ride through Central Park.

Patty Edwards arrived at the chapel a half-hour early. She was the bride-to-be. "I have this bad feeling something is going to go wrong."

"Yes," her mother Jenna said "Today you are a blushing bride to be and the most beautiful bride I have ever seen. "Francis James, the groom-to-be, will be waiting at the altar for you, my child."

"I know that, Mother. All the missing pieces of the puzzle of my life be put into place and be completed." Patty implied for the first time ever her life would come together. This was her big dream, to get married and have a family.

Sitting and fuming with her inner self, she felt trouble in her soul. "I think I'm going to vomit." Her knees buckled as she ran to the ladies room. "I feel safe here," said Patty, smoothing her beautiful white lace and pearl covered long flowing wedding dress which was fit for a princess. Taking a deep breath and preparing herself to say "I do" she smashed into the door when opening it. "This is not good, not good at all."

Everyone wanted to see her get married, friends and family, but her spirit was crushed with all the well wishers that surrounded her. "I have gone this far, my family and friends they are all here." With a frown on her face, "next step, walking down the aisle and taking my vows but first I must release this doubt in my mind."

Slowly walking to the music of the bridal march down the aisle, she mysteriously heard her own voice speaking to her. Listen to your heart. Francis has a secret. The words penetrated deep in her soul. You have problems, girl, big ones. Things aren't always what they appear to be.

Francis stood at the altar in his designer tuxedo, waiting for Patty to stand by his side. The chapel was decorated white gardenias, Patty's favorite flowers. Everyone turned to watch her as she walked down the aisle but she kept asking, What is the secret? She wanted to know before it was too late. In her mind she backtracked when they met to this present day. Francis stood smiling and happy as a lark, as handsome as the day they met on her grand-father's ranch in Houston, Texas. Francis was visiting with Patty's cousin Hunter who lived in the Bronx and worked in Manhattan for an insurance company when she was introduced to him. Father Morex said, "Speak now or forever hold your peace," when the chapel doors flew open. In walked a young man and a pregnant girl. "Stop! News flash! I have plenty to say," the young man said, waving his finger back and forth. "Time to confess your sins, lover boy."

"Yes," the girl added, "caught you in the act, hubby"

"Lover boy! Hubby! I want to say this is kind of off the wall," said Patty.

"We are doing you a favor, when you hear what we have to say," said the young woman. She went on to explain she had been married to Francis for over a year and they were expecting their first child in November. "He is making a mockery out of you."

"I don't believe you," Patty said. "You have to be dis-illusioned and downright Insane."

To which the young girl replied, "Go on, ask Francis," but before Patty opened her mouth the young man said, "Move out of the way, girl. He is mine. We have been seeing each other for the past three months."

"What?" shouted the girl and Patty. "Tell them, Francis, about last night, the passionate time we had like pigeons."

"You bastard," said Patty. "You betrayed me and the love I have for you. You lied when you said you loved me. I have you." She was really going off on him. "This freeway is closed," with a snap of her head, "please turn left and make a detour to the next exit, leave the state line, it's over," looking over her shoulder, pushing it back and forth, "no fly-by-night trip on this freeway anymore!" Then she let out the loudest, longest scream anyone had ever heard, falling on her knees, "No! No! No!"

Jenna tried to comfort her daughter but Patty fainted. John, her father, pointed at Francis signaling him to come and grabbed him by the collar and shook him so hard everyone thought he was going to pop Francis's neck from his spine. Then he punched him in his jaw so that he fell to the floor and began cursing and kicking Francis in his groin and butt. John said, "I'll keep kicking your butt until my foot comes through your mouth. You will not know which end is up. You dirty shameless man." The young man and the girl joined in beating up Francis. "We will kick you straight into next week," the girl said. "You lying cheating dog, I wish we had never met." Then the young man took Francis by the foot, dragging him down the aisle singing "Here Comes the Groom, All Bashed Up In sight," through the chapel doors. Outside he threw Francis over his shoulders then tossed him in the back seat of his convertible, driving off leaving the young girl in tears running after the car.

Back inside the chapel Patty's maid of honor called 911. She was taken to the emergency center where she was diagnosed with lupus.

When the secrets of the past come out the soul will guide you to the right path and true love without the mind games.

Chapter 24

Running Away

When words can longer cover up the pain and the willpower is strong to stay but it's easier to run, running from life is running from one's soul. Augustus Roxstan, a man who honors his words, has a dark side not even his friends know about. His colorful past which came back to bite him hard. Walking in the darkest cloud for many years, believing the wrong his mother Roxanne did to him was intentional when she abandoned him as a baby.

The tragedy unfolded at the mall when an old woman dropped her purse. He picked it up and handed it to her. Noticing she could hardly hold the purse, they befriended each other. One day she invited him to her house, one thing led to another and he found out that the woman was his aunt. "What madness are you talking?" His eyes popping and holding his graze, unimpressed, murmuring, "I guess you never know whom you will meet." There was a great deal of pain in her eyes. Aunt Medi blamed herself for not knowing what her sister Roxanne was doing and why. Also what danger was lurking in her baby's future. She had no clue as to what faced her sister's child at the time.

Roseanne did the best to protect her child from being offered up as a sacrifice from the family of her son's family who wanted more wealth than what they already had. In order to receive more they had to offer up a three-day-old baby. That was the family's belief, for centuries ago it was done in many families. Augustus said to his aunt, "You don't want to go down that road again."

"I have to," his aunt said. "The wrist of the baby had to be slashed allowing the blood to drain into a clay jar."

"I told you don't go that way, but you don't want to listen!" Augustus shouted.

Aunt Medi's voice was a weak whisper. "Inside of the jar there was money, gold, silver, and grains. The jar had to be shaken for three days when the sun is

rising. Then the baby had to be anointed with oil and wrapped in white linen for three days with the sunlight shinning on the mummified body and then the wealth would grow."

His aunt Medi fell on her knees begging forgiveness for her sister Roseanne who was killed after her in-laws found out she gave the baby away to someone from another country. "I have running away from this all my life and now I finally found the way out from walking in the mist." They are all lost in the mist of the dark cloud searching but there will be no way out if you have stepped out of your soul into the darkness.

Stepping into the light that is waiting this was his new dawn. Augustus and his aunt spent the rest of the day talking. It had been a very long and difficult journey for Medi Fern. Finally the devastating tragedy was told. She apologized once more, expressing her heartfelt sorrows to her nephew. He was frustrated and punched the air as he paced across the floor as a wrench wheel whisper, trying to shake the image of what his aunt had told him about his past. "I can't let this take over my life by being afraid and running away," her nephew told her. Medi also told Augustus about a vision she had when she was eighteen. At twenty-one years old she babysat four baby girls from two different countries. In her vision one of the baby girls died a horrible death in a car crash with her mother and that girl's soul was reincarnated as her own baby girl some years later. Also Medi saw her soul visit a place in heaven. Somewhere in a garden a group of baby girls sat on the bank of a stream. The water glittered as gold glitters and a ray of sunlight reflected on it. One of the baby girls said to her, "We have mothers and grandmothers here who wait for us. We are very happy here." All the babies looked like cherubs. For Medi her spirit had revived and she could go to sleep at night without tunning from her soul. To put an end to her pain she had to go back and relive the beginning. No need for her to feel like running away in a hole as rats do when seen or heard.

Part 2

They lived below the poverty line scraping to live one day at a time. They drank cups of hot tea and ate bread sometimes with butter and cheese or cereal with water and sugar that had to last them until the next meal. Dinner was rice and peas or beans, water or lemonade to drink for months. They dreaded summer time and were scared to go outside for fear that others would laugh at them, which they did. Wearing the same clothes year in and year out, their mother's paycheck went into paying bills and rent. Many times they faced eviction but God always sent help in time so they could have enough. Their mother worked from Sunday to Sunday, not remembering what day of the month it was at the time. In her pocket book (handbag) all she had was twenty-five cents to make a phone call if needed. Her minimum wages were not enough to feed chickens for a week. She carried a bottle of boiled water, a book to read, a notebook to write in. She did not even have lunch. The same thing she ate for breakfast she ate when she got home from work. She usually washed her hands and thanked God she made it, ate her bread, and drank her tea or coffee without sugar while looking around to scrape up something for dinner. She always found something to put together. No one knew how she put things together but she did and made a meal. Most of the time she kept a pack of chewing gum. When she felt hungry at work she would cut one stick of gum in half, leaving the other half for another day. That was her lunch for months.

Two of her friends helped them out at times. One friend didn't have much but what little she had she shared between them. Her two friends looked out for them when no one else would, no family did. Everyone turned away from them because they were very poor and she was a single parent. Their mother always said to them things would get better someday. Hold on to your faith and everything would turn around. Nothing lasts forever. God only gives what one can bear. We have each other, truth, and love. Life will not always be this way. No need for us to keep running away from the truth. This is what is and where we are, so let us think about where we are going and keep our focus there, okay, my children. When we get out of this we will be better, stronger people, living a better life style. She had never taken a vacation and always took a back seat to make sure they had something to keep them going. It was a painful cycle with all the pressure for their family to undergo. She was exhausted to her bones from not getting any rest and was short-tempered with the children. She needed some downtime for herself but when would that be?

They appreciated what she was doing and valued these life experiences but it was unfortunate that they had to live a life like this. When they knew she was hurting and as a lawn needs water to grow so did their mother need rest to focus. She hope that one day they would know what it felt like not being scared to open the door when the bell rang, hoping it was not the rent office. When their anxiety peaked what they had been keeping inside started to fester and stew in the moments when they worried about tomorrow and the next day. Realizing they didn't know everything she had in her head but one thing they did know, they were like sticks in a bundle and that made them stronger in these uncertain times in their lives, watching their mother struggling with everything instead of stopping and enjoying life.

Part 3

Taylor Nuke is a man who ran from his responsibilities. He ran from fatherhood, from relationships, and anything that stared him in the face. When he was a young man all he wanted to do was have fun with a variety of women, never taking things seriously, always on defense. He impressed everyone with his handsome face and dashing smile but he needed to do some soul searching or get beaten to a pulp to come to his senses.

The guy had the nerve to back out on his family for many years. Now Taylor wanted to be close, just like a puppy jumping all over them. He didn't value them before, why now? Promising to give them what they needed, when they needed it, but when time came for him to put up once again love jumped out of the window. Help went with it. Taylor went running away his words were, "I can't help myself right now, far more to help anybody else." He ran as if his spirit within him was running after him fast and hard. Suddenly they became anybody. He took the phone from his ear, handed it to one of his buddies, and that was the end of the conversion. The last they heard from him, the phone calls stopped coming.

Asking for help sounded like some cocktail party nonsense to both of them. Neither believed that this was happening but in fact it was. How could one love someone one minute and leave them the next. Running from your own family because they asked for help, a place to live, and food to eat? Turning his back and the screw tighter as he turned away from them again. For Taylor it was fast, safe, and painless. That saved him. It would darken the sky for him if he had to provide quality of life for them. One can never forget the look an Johnnathan's face when he hung up the phone. The face of grief had a silent voice, in that moment, his eyes brimming with tears of sorrow, his eyes gazing to the floor, he was ashamed of his father. He stood motionless.

Chapter 25

Second Chance

((Wow, everyone wants a second chance, so stop belly aching and acting as a damn roadrunner running up and down after Ryan."

"Whatever," Kimberly said, Erin's plea was thrown right back at her with laughter. Their friendship was forged in a time of their own personal crisis. That kind of bonded friendship can really never be broken. When life for them was dark their friendship gave them a flicker or light and hope. "Don't you ever, ever question my love for Ryan again, for crying out loud. Go back to your cooking, Erin."

"Kimberly, you know what I'm saying is true."

"Oh! Gosh! I don't want to hear that crap over and over again; he is not good enough for me. That I deserve better. Shut up. Ryan wants a second chance. I think it's light for me to give him the benefit of the doubt. Don't you think so, friend."

"I don't enjoy this," she said "but I feel you're stepping out of line now. As painful as it is please stay out of my life. You will hurt yourself, do you get that," Erin said, "oh!"

Kim answered, "Erin, put two and two together. He hurt you, lied to you and cheated on you. I have watched you cry for many days, seen the hurt in your eyes, knowing Ryan is in New Jersey in her apartment. His priority lies with you but he is giving it to her. I'm concerned about your happiness. We're best friends." "Kimberly, it's frustrating seeing you so hurt and angry most of the time. We need each other. It's a mess. the only way to get a handle on it is to speak to Ryan. Tell him what you think of him and why? And while you're at it, girl, let him know what you need from him."

"Stop blaming yourself by finding reasons for what he has done. He has to take responsibility for his own actions. Think about now and the hereafter. If you can get over these obstacles and still want to give him a second chance it's up to you, Kimberly. You're a beautiful young woman. Ryan is only your boyfriend, not your husband. To be honest with you I think you should date others. It's not as if a soup stain is on your blouse that can't be removed, girl, is it?"

Kimberly replied. "I'm sick and tired of hearing you yapping about what's what. May all this talking stop please? Are you going to continue until the sun begins to rise high in the sky, Erin? What about your relationship with Abram? You bent over backwards for his family so that they would like you, that I do know. They didn't like you from the get go. What in the hell makes you think they will like you now?"

Kimberly said with a harsh tone in her voice to her friend Erin, "as the waves of the ocean rise, rolls and then falls before it break on the shore, so is the relationship between Abram's family. You are their suck up. They kiss up and pretend when they want something from you. do you let them use you? They badmouth you all the time.

"Abram is a broke joker. He doesn't have a job. Girl, don't be as a school of fishes swimming in the same direction looking for an escape from the sharks."

"What, am I fish food, Kim?" Erin shouted at her. Kimberly didn't listen. She went on to say, "Remember the tide comes in and goes out. The kind of liking Abram's family has for you, it comes and goes."

His mother once said as the sun descended in the horizon, she would see to it that the relationship her son had with that Erin ended. What did he see in that girl? Kim overheard Abram's mother's conversation one day talking about Erin.

Erin spun around and slapped Kim in her face. The aroma of baked potatoes and roast beef filled the air. "Kimberly, what is it going to be, you witch?" Erin turned to walk away but Kimberly grabbed and tugged on her arm. "You witch, either you stop this or I'll beat the crap out of you."

Erin pushed Kimberly to the floor, she got up grabbed the broom and whacked Erin on her foot. They both started kicking and screaming, pulling and tugging on each other's hair, scratching each other's eyes and face, biting and ripping into one another with their long fingernails, rolling on the floor, knocking over everything in their path. "You're the worst of human nature. Where is your soul?" Kimberly said.

Erin replied, "You took it from me when you slept with my boyfriend in high school."

Kimberly yelled. "Maybe you should have been much nicer to him when you were seeing each other then. Huh! You always said a girl should never settle for less but for the best and he was the best."

Bang with a frying pan on Erin's head, punching her with her fist in her side, Kim laughed. They were fighting like mad dogs.

In walked Abram. "What's all this rated R stuff going on in here?" He looked at them. "Ain't this sad. Stop!" they heard Abram shout. "Get away from her. What is the matter with you all? Is this the way best friends carry on. Are you two going mad? The fighting stopped abruptly.

"Why are you all blowing out so much steam on each other?" Abram said. "Clean up the garbage in your lives beginning within yourselves."

Bewildered by Abram's remarks Kimberly replied, "I got to get out of here. Let me out of here, please."

Abram went on to say, "This was heading for a dangerous situation. throwing away your friendship. Please remember the way things were before all this, I'd like to remind you that this type of thing is considered inappropriate behavior. If both of you need to hash things out this wasn't a good strategy, girls. Erin, it was stupid tackling Kim down to the floor." Abram made his point very clear and went on to say his mother always told him the deepest longing a woman could ever have is loneliness. "The deepest pain is the loss of a child, the lost of friendship, or a long relationship that ended suddenly. Was risking this friendship so important? What happened here? Take a look at how it would be like living the next few days without your friendship. Give each other a second chance and try to improve your friendship. It would be a doggone shame to become enemies. Think about it. Erin. say what is in your heart and soul. Tell Kim how you really feel about what happened here today and her friendship with you. Forgive each other." Abram held his hands in a prayer position. "Please, Lord, let them become friends again."

After two days Erin thought renewing their friendship by giving it a second chance would be a blessing. She called Kimberly. "Hello Kim, this is Erin," "What is it Erin? I don't want to leave this dangling between us any longer."

"What?" asked Kimberly.

"It was no coincidence that this happened, on second thought maybe we should meet in person and talk things over and give each other a second chance."

Kim answered, "Why not? we have been friends most of our lives and should remain real with one another despite what went down with us. That was a bitter-sweet day. life is short."

"I totally agree," Erin replied. "It was only past pain that set off things and no one will come close to having the type of friendship we had together. Please forgive me for any wrongdoing. I'm confident it's going to work out. What I am asking you to do is to put what happened out of your mind. Take into consideration all the good and wonderful times we had together we should be grateful for those times." She began to cry.

Kimberly said, "We are not going to make that mistake again. Do you forgive me, Erin?"

"I had forgiven you before you asked for forgiveness. Hey let's hang together tomorrow at the shopping mall and talk some more. I want to get you a peace offering. See you later, aside from me beating you up, you are a good person and friend. I feel somehow more connected to you and it's from my heart. Nevertheless, bye."

Erin and Kimberly had become friends in kindergarten. When Kim's mother died six months later, every lunch time Erin would go over to Kim's lunch table to sit with her, their friendship developed into a sisterly love, big sister looking out for little sister. Giving someone a second chance is soulful and smart, for some day we will want a second chance from someone. Most of the time the result is compelling if it is from one's soul, reaching deep into the soul is a dreamlike experience.

Chapter 26

Helping Hands

Stretch forth your hands and wash them with milk and honey. Children, we got dinner tonight and plenty. What about those who have nothing, not even a place to sleep tonight or tomorrow night? The skies are blue with sunlight, starlight tonight. Your heart is without light or a starry night. When the moon shines tomorrow night it will be the light in your souls. It will be bright and so will be your universe. No wondering eyes or telling lies, any dark-circled eyes to crusty mouth.

Stretch forth your hand for the fruit of life, a taste of this, a taste of that, sugary taste, salty, bitter, not so sweet, taste the joy, the we all know and taste in life, every life. Will tomorrow come? Is yesterday really gone? What about today, is it really here or was it yesterday? Maybe it is tomorrow. What about today? Do you know yesterday is today and tomorrow is the same? What you did yesterday most of it you will repeat today and tomorrow over and over. The same time yesterday, today and tomorrow will be the same twelve A.M. and tomorrow twelve A.M. time. Look closer, yes, you. Seeking out the good in will help us keep our promises. We can be forgiving of others and ourselves, When we welcome friends we welcome life.

Open hands, helping hands, helping the angels with delight. Dew drop dries, tear drops dry, so will the tears in your eyes tonight. When a rainbow appears the sky will be happy with the color blue and not green. Red will bleed in the heart of the believers for passion of life and love. Yellow for success one may achieve if you believe in yourself. Green for prosperity that awaits in this universe if we listen to the cry of our souls when tears flood our hearts. White clouds are the tender giving purity from our souls. Black nights are the darkness, which lurks in corners of our souls. Behind darkness comes the light of goodness that our hearts may be inspired by spiritual upliftment from helping hands. When you give a helping hand, it is like a footprint in the sand. It gives you joy, it gives you pleasure and peace within your soul.

Part 2

Respect the spirit within you. In return it will treat you with respect. If one humbles and surrenders before the most holy high one, which is God the father, he will grant us the life that is really ours. When we bow unto the Almighty father as low as we can he will lift us up as high as a mountain. He gave us eyes that we may see, ears that we may hear, a nose to smell and a tongue to taste and to speak wisdom and understanding with, touch that one can feel and sense the presence of the pure holy ones. He gave us a helping hand. Hold on to his unchanging love.

When a child is born it is helpless, as it grows you teach the child how to clap, to talk, dance, walk, and run. You give that child a helping hand. Everyone needs a helping hand at some point in time in their lives. When we see someone who really needs a helping hand, stretch forth and give help no matter how small it may be. To that family, child, man, woman, old, or young, let it come from the corner of your soul. It will be a blessing in your life in days to come. What about the family who has to be bouncing from place to place, never having, never knowing when? Where or if they are going to have somewhere to call their own. Some people wherever they go it only for a little while the questions continue in their minds.

What price do we have to pay to stay here? Is it worth it? Could we measure up to their lifestyle? Everyone feels disconnected from what they knew and had before when their inner voice whispers. Is there any satisfaction in being here and what is its purpose? For a minute you can say we are sure you enjoy your stay here, make yourselves at home. Then one day you say goodbye, thank you for allowing us to stay here and for offering us a place to stay, but it's time for us to leave now. God's blessing and thank you again, picking up their last bundle of stuff maybe in a shopping bag, a black garbage bag, or a traveling bag someone gave them, fighting back the tears, turning around slowly, not wanting to show. Waving goodbye as a member of their family, say we know this was only temporary, what lessons we learned from this will stay with us forever.

No more making telephone calls relating our experiences to others; there's no rejecting calls, no call waiting, no home voice mail, or mail box message, no billing date, no dial tone, we have no phone. Appreciate what blessings we have in our lives. Remember, everything we do contributes to either improve or destroy our lives. Searching your soul for the kindness within will brightly burn the flame that flickers within; no harmful thoughts. See the vision within as it reveals the passion of giving, embracing our spirits, enlighten our knowledge by connecting the dots. When giving a helping hand in life we all will be tested along the way. It's up to us the individual to know which way we must go, what's right and what's not. There will be many temptations in disguise as we travel life's pathway; there be honey, maple ham, lions and lambs, vinegar and wine, but know which is the thirst quencher. Open your eyes as you drink from the cup. Don't turn away from the weary eyes that stare in your face.

Happiness comes, happiness goes, and helping hands come and go. Memories stay, good or bad. Its imprints stay on one's soul. When our time here on this earth is very limited, give with your heart a helping hand. Be tough, be strong, have faith, my child. Dry your tears and say your prayers. Say good night, then go to sleep.

Chapter 27

Silence of the Night

In the middle of the night to watch the souls of men grow, as we sleep our souls grow like a plant and blooms as a rose that in the garden of the gods and the holy heavenly beings. The silent fragrant garden is filled with eternally scented jasmine, lilies, geranium, roses, etc. Follow the fragrance where the wind blows and you will find the gods and heavenly beings who like that scented rose.

Silent feelings flow and my soul flies, no shell of a human body to protect or hold back my feelings, no world as my soul rides the chariot of eternal love. Oh Star of David that shines on me and those like me, you leave your mark for all to see. No worldly love could ever compensate for the eternal love that flows in our souls and the lily scent that lingers when the wind blows. The holy heavenly beings are interested in the human body; the only use of the body they have is to dwell in, to house, to shelter, to manifest carrying out their works. They are holy beings of light that have completed their life missions here on earth. They are only after our spirits and souls, preparing the chosen ones to educate and to share their wisdom, knowledge, and compassion with this world.

Everyone we come in contact with or are drawn to was meant to be. Every path we take in our lives was meant to be that way. We learn and grow from each other's experiences, wisdom, and understanding. As our souls grow and our spirits become stronger in the silence of the night, it travels as lightning flashing. As it whips by, a flash of light here or there, that's what our worldly eyes may see.

Part 2

When we sleep at night a world rises up in the universe and our world goes to sleep. Our naked eyes were made to see on world, this world, and it is not what it seems at night. When the sun sets unsupernatural world rises. This cycle goes on and on. Do you ever wonder when the darkness falls and all is asleep what really goes on in the unseen world? One thing, this world goes on forever, world without end, only the living human beings and other life forms perish from this world then new life forms begin. There is no yesterday, today, and tomorrow. Our eyes and minds were made to see and think the way we do. Remember, this is a world of karma and reincarnation, a cleansing world for our souls. It's a passage to the many worlds of the gods and only one true world of the highest, God Almighty. No one is above him, only beneath him.

Part 3

As the spirit world awakens, the gods of heaven are out passing by and the evil spirits that roam this earth wait for the shadows of the gods. In the darkness they move like thieves in the silence of the night when they know our souls are out searching for God's wisdom and our spirits are unguarded. Evil spirits move in to trap us as we sleep, tempting, feeding on our weaknesses and our fears to steal our very souls if we let them.

When souls are trapped in this dimension they fight to become free that they may sail and float to find their way to their homes, fighting against dark evil spirits. When our world sleeps, evil invades our dreams, pulling and sucking the energy from our spirits as we sleep. Good souls who are trapped in this dimension search for human bodies who may be worthy of their souls, then house within them, guiding, protecting, and helping our human spirit grow stronger spiritually.

Evil or bad souls search for people whose characters are more like their own, dwelling within their host, speaking, and calling their victims to follow their ways. If one's spirit is weak it can easily be pulled to the dark side. Dark forces are barracudas. They prey on souls. Souls that are good help like friends do by signaling something is wrong, fighting, pulling us out of the darkness into the light. While heavenly forces and the gods are always looking out, fighting the battle against darkness and the evil forces of this world and the spirit world to save our souls.

Chapter 28

Beyond

Beyond the big blue sky there are valleys and mountains, bridges and tunnels, the city beyond the sky. There is a burst of air, a burst of bubbles where our souls belong. Our body is a product of this world. We breathe the air of this universe, walk the earth, sleep, and talk but our existence is limited here. Most souls are from ancient times passing through, walking the path of their journey with the past and present on both side and the memories of yesterday bound behind them. Ahead their way is clear. Souls ride the waves sailing into the city beyond the blue sky, a higher dimension a high level; no one takes anything with them, there is no place that need it. Needs and wants are of this material world. Up there all that is needed is the eternal feeling of everlasting love. When we breathe the air it is always light. Souls float gently passing by, silently whispering God's praises.

For there's a path beyond the sea where the waves whisper and the crowned cheer. Souls gather as you go down with one hand, pointing downwards, circling as a fish to meet the middle then come up with both hands pointing upward. There is a world many don't know exists where there are living, breathing, holy beings. There are planets in this universe that men will never find, reach, or see. planets or the gods, planets of the angels, planets of the saints. They all keep watch over us in the silence of the night.

There is the God of gods, souls of souls, and kingdoms of kingdoms. Chariots of fire, chariots of love, and chariots of wisdom. There is a higher level of wisdom in the great kingdom of God where his angels sit at his feet as he stretches forth his hands to every soul.

Part 2

He spoke to us from the mountaintop, from bridges and plains to the banks of the rivers, in The ditches by the bay he called us out from hiding. He gave us the gift of light and darkness, day and night, that we might choose the way to the light or the way to darkness. He gave us the sound of thunder and lightning to make music. He gave unto this world and all life forms yet we are not satisfied.

Oh Holy One as you come to us, let us feel your presence as Moses did in the land of Egypt so we can tell the stories to this world that you live. God lives and his holy powers live. They are greater and stronger than any of the manmade laws of this world. When he stands on the mountaintop the world will hear his voice. Our world has been asleep for a long time. It's time to wake up, world, come out, come out of our caves and holes and lift up our heads high to the sky. All of this dimension must remember that what is here is only for this world, only for a moment. It glitters as gold and rubies and can be melted into dust. We must not step on the poor and needy, using them like washcloths, then tossing them aside.

There is only one true throne, the heavenly king, one true crown made of gold with stars and myrrh embedded into it. Who wears that crown? The Almighty, leader of leaders, king of kings, and God of all gods, God of the higher dimensions and this world and all worlds. One day he will wake up our spirits in the land of the living and the land of the dead. We walk among the dead; we walk side by side with them because we have not freed them from this world. We bound them here and torment our world with so much darkness. We bury our dead so deep into the earth their spirits can't sail and their souls can't fly to find their place of rest. We make it hard for the living and the dead. Weeping for the dead? Weep for ourselves, our children, and the living for the wrong we have done by burying our dead too deep into the earth. They will always be trapped here; our tears will be of no use to them. Let their spirits sail and their souls fly. Free ourselves and the world from mournful cries of the souls in the silence of the night. Awake! For the time has come for us to walk into the light of wisdom. The life of the soul is a cycle with no end, only rebirth.

Chapter 29

Hallelujah!

We shall sing the songs of praise of the Almighty God from whence he came, in ancient times to present times, in times to come, which is the everlasting time that will live on. His name will give new life and new meaning to this world. His miracles will be performed in front of the eyes of men, women, and children. When the time comes the tongues of some will be shaped as a serpent, the words of others will flow as a passing breeze on the tips of their tongue. They will speak of visions of things to come. In the open fields every eye will be open looking up to heaven, every hand shall stretch forth, and every knee shall bend. Holy messengers will come to us with visions of creatures crawling out of the sea by night, some will be going back, digging deep into the past for ancient herbs, healing with better understanding and willingness to learn the secrets of ancient medicine. When all the gods and angels are called upon to sit around the Almighty father's throne, this cycle of life will end and a new cycle of life will begin unfolding in mystical ways just like a rose.

Part 2

Our soul is like a rose; it grows, blooms, and then opens. When the soul is opened in full, it is awakened with wisdom our worldly belief. When souls cry they are calling out to the Lord for his mercy and blessing upon us with the hand of his rod that we may understand what eternal life means.

A soul glows. it sparkles, twinkling in the light of day, and by night it lights up the darkness. The heavenly gods souls twinkle, sending down their glow to our souls, feeding knowledge into our souls with mystical visions. They want us to know and to share with this divine universe that we may not go on living in darkness and ignorance, that we may see this world in new eyes from our souls. Given from our souls not to gain worldly treasures but to gain a place in his kingdom, the souls of children grow while middle-aged and older people experience more wisdom, understanding, and a calmer, gentler spirit, which glows from our souls. The souls of children are innocent; they play like a harp with every string of the soul, so pure, so giving, loving and sweet.

Part 3

When the spirit and the soul enter into our bodies at birth it makes us into a living, breathing human being, it makes us come alive to breathe, to live, and to think. It becomes one with our body, the gift of life, to love, and to feel. At birth whatever soul and spirit we get, that is who we become in this life. The souls and spirits that are waiting in the mystical world play and make friends like children do here on earth, forming bonds with each other, making attachment to other souls. The older souls create friendships and fall in love. In mystical ways the intense force of energy emerges from one soul and spirit to another when they enter into this world. The souls and spirits that are supposed to live for a long time find each other wherever they are born.

When souls romance in the mystical spirit world they float and their spirits fly. Some sail by twinkling around each other with flashing beans of glowing lights of green, yellow, white, and red. A green glow happens when souls are alert and fall in love. Yellow glow means think before acting, white glow means this soul is the one, red glow, this soul is not for me, move on. They twinkle as stars in the sky at night. They let out sweet fragrance, which smells like perfume. The scent of the soul connects with another soul in the spirit world, following that soul wherever it goes and claims that soul as its own soul mate for the mystical world and the physical world.

Human beings flirt and hold hands with each other, pair up. In the mystical world of spiritual beings their souls flirt and they do pair up. The energy from their souls are so vibrant, energetic, and exciting, the juices flow as they dash by one another, letting out their sweet scented fragrance from their souls. One can hear the joyous laughter.

When souls are romancing the glowing energy sparks love with the sound of music from their souls; the intense magnetic force pulls each soul interlocking the hearts of their souls together in the spirit world. When the souls enter this physical world their souls are still interlocked and they find each other when the time is right, no matter where they were born or come from. The souls who find their soulmates in this world, a part of their soul's memory remembers the twinkling feeling it felt life times ago when their souls were romancing in the mystical spiritual world.

One will know when you have found each other again because it is felt deep within our souls. That is when the soul is talking to our hearts with the same twinkling glow and intense magnetic force, the feeling of love and the sweet fragrant scent that the soul remembers. Each soul has its own unique personality. When souls are in love they can become jealous, obsessive, possessive, and protective in the supernatural world, just like us human beings in this world. We become them when in love and just like the lily of the valley, we need each other to survive and to stay alive.